C000170797

# *The*
# HIDDEN PLACES
## *of*
# SUSSEX

*Edited by*
*Barbara Vesey*

Published by:

Travel Publishing Ltd

7a Apollo House, Calleva Park

Aldermaston, Berks, RG7 8TN

ISBN 1-902-00709-3

© Travel Publishing Ltd 1998

| | |
|---|---|
| *First Published:* | *1993* |
| *Second Edition:* | *1995* |
| *Third Edition:* | *1998* |

## Regional Titles in the Hidden Places Series:

| | |
|---|---|
| Channel Islands | Cheshire |
| Cornwall | Devon |
| Dorset, Hants & Isle of Wight | Gloucestershire |
| Heart of England | Kent |
| Lake District & Cumbria | Lancashire |
| Norfolk | Northeast Yorkshire |
| Northumberland & Durham | Nottinghamshire |
| Peak District | Potteries |
| Somerset | South East |
| South Wales | Suffolk |
| Surrey | Sussex |
| Thames & Chilterns | Welsh Borders |
| Wiltshire | Yorkshire Dales |

## National Titles in the Hidden Places Series:

| | |
|---|---|
| England | Ireland |
| Scotland | Wales |

Printing by: Nuffield Press, Abingdon

Cartography by: Estates Publications, Tenterden, Kent

Line Drawings: Sarah Bird

Editor: Barbara Vesey

Cover : Clare Hackney

Born in 1961, Clare was educated at West Surrey College of Art and Design as well as studying at Kingston University. She runs her own private water-colour school based in Surrey and has exhibited both in the UK and internationally. The cover is taken from an original water-colour of the village of Bosham.

# Foreword

**The Hidden Places** series is a collection of easy to use travel guides taking you, in this instance, on a relaxed but informative tour of Sussex - a county rich in heritage and endowed with rolling hills and spectacular natural beauty as well as a charming and picturesque coastline. Our books contain a wealth of interesting information on the history, the countryside, the towns and villages and the more established places of interest in the county. But they also promote the more secluded and little known visitor attractions and places to stay, eat and drink many of which are easy to miss unless you know exactly where you are going.

We include hotels, inns, restaurants, public houses, teashops, various types of accommodation, historic houses, museums, gardens, garden centres, craft centres and many other attractions throughout Sussex. Most places have an attractive line drawing and are cross-referenced to coloured maps found at the rear of the book. We do not award merit marks or rankings but concentrate on describing the more interesting, unusual or unique features of each place with the aim of making the reader's stay in the local area an enjoyable and stimulating experience.

Whether you are visiting Sussex for business or pleasure or in fact are living in the county we do hope that you enjoy reading and using this book. We are always interested in what readers think of places covered (or not covered) in our guides so please do not hesitate to use the reader reaction forms provided to give us your considered comments. We also welcome any general comments which will help us improve the guides themselves. Finally if you are planning to visit any other corner of the British Isles we would like to refer you to the list of other **Hidden Places** titles to be found at the rear of the book.

# Contents

# CHAPTER ONE
## Chichester & The West Sussex Coast

*Bosham across the water*

# Chapter 1 - Area Covered

*For precise location of places please refer to the colour maps found at the rear of the book.*

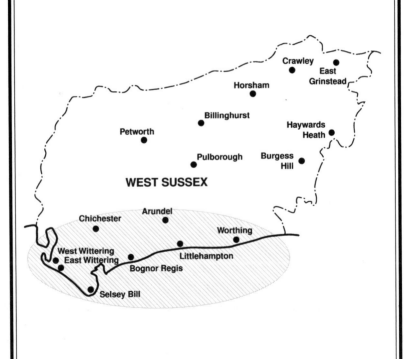

# 1
# Chichester & The West Sussex Coast

## Introduction

Sun, sand and surf - the West Sussex landscape around Chichester is typified by small, pastoral towns and seacoast villages. This is also rural river country, a haven for wildfowl and home to some lovely stately manors, gardens and other and rural retreats.

Chichester, with its stunning cathedral and castle, is a cultural centre of the region, offering a renowned English theatre and, in summer, the *'Chichester Festivities'* - an international festival of music and the arts. On a clear day, if you're not at nearby Goodwood horse racing track, you can see Chichester's ancient cathedral from out on the water. The justly renowned Chichester Harbour is a lively centre for boating and watersports, a haven for all boat lovers and yachtsmen. At nearby Itchenor, waterborne tours of Chichester Harbour are available throughout the year.

The South Downs between Chichester and the English Channel repay exploration with panoramic views and peaceful bucolic scenes. The villages of Chilgrove, West Dean and Singleton offer pleasant walking or touring and some excellent country inns. West Dean is also home to handsome public gardens containing many old rose species; just one of the many fine gardens in the area. Singleton is an attractive community in the valley of the River Lavant. At historic Fishbourne, visitors will find the site of the largest non-military Roman building yet to be uncovered in Britain.

The very attractive village of Bosham is said to be the site of King Canute's failed attempt to make the sea retreat on command. Apuldram is a charming place on the Chichester Channel with a number of fascinating places to visit, including a 13th-century church and several waterside pubs. Here can also be found a magnificent 15th-century manor house. The pleasant, peaceful community of Sidlesham and its neighbour, Pagham, are the centres for a fascinating wildlife sanctuary. The coastal beaches at West Wittering and Selsey combine a plethora of things to do with relative tranquillity and the space to delve into all manner of leisure pursuits.

Bognor Regis, Littlehampton and Worthing and Shoreham-by-Sea on the Channel coast became popular resorts during the 18th-century 'sea bathing' craze. In Bognor, bathers have since made room for late-20th-century windsurfers. The nearby village centre of Felpham was once home to poet William Blake, and now features popular pubs, restaurants and shops. This part of West Sussex, its gentle pleasures and diversions, is a true haven for those seeking a picturesque seaside or countryside break.

# Chichester

Chichester, the ancient county town of West Sussex, was founded by the Romans in the 1st century AD. Set on low-lying plains between the coast and the wooded South Downs, the city walls and four major thoroughfares - North, East, South and West Streets - follow the original Roman plan, criss-crossing at the spot where the fine 16th-century Butter Cross now stands. This ornate 50-foot octagonal edifice was built in 1500 by Bishop Edward Story to provide shelter for the many traders who came to ply their wares at the city's busy market.

The invading Roman legions used Chichester as a base camp, christening it *Noviomagus*, the 'new city of the plain'. The city's modern name is derived from Cissa's ceaster (or castle) after the Saxon King Cissa, who ruled this part of Sussex around 500 AD.

The city walls, constructed around 200 AD, originally consisted of raised earthwork embankments built in an irregular 11 sided polygon. Alterations and improvements proceeded over the next few centuries; today the city walls date back primarily to medieval times, as can be seen in the large sections that remain on the boundary of the old city. Modern Chichester is home to some first-rate examples of Georgian architecture and town planning. It is a charming and enjoyable place to explore.

Chichester has a long and colourful ecclesiastical history. Although St Wilfrid chose nearby Selsey as the site of the area's first cathedral in the 8th century, the conquering Normans decided to build a new cathedral in its present location at the end of the 11th century. Situated near the corner of West and South streets, the ***Cathedral*** rests on Roman foundations. Construction began in 1091; the new cathedral was finally consecrated in 1184. Three years later, however, it was almost totally destroyed by fire. The rebuilding programme was undertaken in the 13th century by Richard of Chichester, a venerated bishop who was canonised in 1262 and subsequently adopted as the town's patron saint.

***Chichester Cathedral***

Chichester Cathedral is unique on two counts: it is the only mediaeval English cathedral which can be seen from the sea - rather than being secluded down its own close, as is more usual for cathedrals of this period - and has a detached belfry. This latter was built because it was feared the existing tower was insufficiently sturdy to hold the cathedral bells, and indeed in 1861 the spire blew down in storm, demolishing a large section of the nave. The present 277 foot spire was designed by preeminent architect Sir Gilbert Scott in keeping with the cathedral's original style, and can been seen for miles around in every direction.

Inside, the cathedral contains some fine Norman arches, a double aisle, a set of 14th century choir stalls and some excellent modern works of art, including an altar tapestry by John Piper, a painting of Christ appearing to Mary Magdalene by Graham Sutherland, and a stained glass window by Marc Chagall. Other treasures include two of the most important Norman sculptures in Britain: *The Raising of Lazarus* and *Christ Arriving in Bethany*, on the south wall, near the altar, and a glass panel revealing a group of Roman mosaics uncovered during restoration in the late 1980s. Guided tours of the cathedral are possible.

**The Prebendal School**, the cathedral choir school and the oldest school in Sussex, stands alongside the main building.

The 13thcentury **St Mary's Hospital** in St Martin's Square off Priory Road has some unique misericords in its chapel, and a pretty walled garden. This worthy establishment is still used to house 'the deserving elderly of the city'. The warden is pleased to show visitors around the chapel and certain parts of the residents' quarters.

Other early buildings in Chichester include **St Olave's Church** in North Street, now a bookshop, and **The Bishop's Palace** (just south of the cathedral), which has delightful and pleasant gardens and a 12th century chapel containing a unique wall painting. (Permission to view this can be obtained from the bishop's office.)

In the post-Roman era, Chichester remained an important administrative centre and market town. Between the 14th and 18th centuries, it was a major trading and exporting centre for the Sussex wool industry, and many handsome merchants' houses remain, especially around St Martin's Square and the elegant Georgian enclave known as The Pallants. **Pallant House** is a fine example of an elegant redbrick town house built in 1713 by the local wine merchant Henry 'Lisbon' Peckham.

The building is guarded by a wonderful pair of carved stone dodos and has an unusual observation tower where the owner would look out for his merchant vessels returning laden with goods from the Iberian Peninsula. The kitchen and furnishings of this fine house are Edwardian. Now restored and refurbished as a gallery, Pallant House is home to a collection of modern British art based around the impressive collection bequeathed to the city by the late Dean Hussey, an acknowledged patron of the arts. Exhibits include a lovely collection of Bow porcelain and some fine example of 20thcentury paintings by artists such as Paul Klee, Fernand Leger, Graham Sutherland and John Piper, as well as regular special exhibitions.

If you are looking for somewhere to stay in Chichester, *Friary Close* is a large Georgian town house situated in a quiet corner of central Chichester. The house dates to about 1810 and is built actu-

*Friary Close*

ally astride the city wall. Unusually for such a central location there is a walled garden, formally laid out, of over half an acre. The three bedrooms are at second-floor level, each with bathroom or shower room ensuite. There is car parking at the premises. No smoking. *Friary Close, Friary Lane, Chichester, West Sussex PO19 1UF Tel: 01243 527294*

Chichester boasts a proud military history and is home to the *Royal Military Police*, or Redcaps, whose museum is open to the public. It can be found on Broyle Road.

One of Chichester's most distinctive modern buildings can be found at Oaklands Park, just north of the city walls. Since the hexagonally shaped *Festival Theatre* was opened in 1962, it has built up an international reputation for staging the finest classical and contemporary drama, opera and ballet. The theatre is one of the focal points of the annual Chichester Festival, a two week programme of cultural events which takes place each July. Festivities include classical concerts in the cathedral and fireworks displays at Goodwood Racecourse. Along with Salisbury and Winchester, Chichester also plays its part in the summer Southern Cathedrals Festival.

The acclaimed **Chichester District Museum** is located in the area of the city known as Little London. This interesting and well laid out museum creates a vivid picture of life in this part of West Sussex from the Stone Age to the present day, along with a fascinating exhibition illustrating the many changes which have affected Chichester during the last 100 years. The museum also contains a special section dedicated to the history of the Royal Sussex Regiment from its foundation in 1701 to the present day. The museum's particularly good collection of Roman relics and artefacts is housed in the interesting former **Guildhall** in Priory Park, which began life as a Grey Friars church in medieval times.

The city is also a haven for all boat lovers and yachtsmen, with a bustling harbour from which you can set off on a boat trip, or alternatively spend some time strolling past some of the fabulous yachts moored in the marina, one of Europe's largest.

The tranquil Summersdale area of Chichester makes for a good base for exploring the town and surrounding area. Tucked away in this quiet part of north Chichester in a sedate and attractive road, **Mrs P M Davenport's** bed and breakfast retreat is ideally situated for Chichester theatre events, coastal drives and country rambles. Summersdale is a haven from the busier parts of Chichester, while still being within convenient distance of all that the region has to offer, including the horse racing and historic motor racing at Goodwood. Mrs Davenport is a charming, happy hostess with a knack for making her guests feel at home. She has useful knowledge of the local area and a keen interest in golf and gardening. The ambience in this charming establish-

*Summersdale*

ment is very cosy and comfortable - a real home from home. Breakfasts are hearty and home-cooked with home-made preserves on the table. *Mrs P M Davenport, 4, The Lane, Summersdale, Chichester, West Sussex PO19 4PY  Tel: 01243 527293.*

# Around Chichester

## Portfield
*Map 1 ref C8*

*1 mile E of Chichester off the A27*

Church Road in Portfield is home to the **Mechanical Music and Doll Collection**, a fascinating museum housed in a former Victorian church. Among the curiosities here are barrel organs, pianolas, fairground organs, phonographs and music boxes. The curators offer regular demonstrations of these rare and historic instruments which are all fully restored and in working order. There is also a collection of over 100 late Victorian china-headed dolls, along with stereoscopes, magic lanterns and a number of related artefacts from the Victorian and Edwardian eras. (Tel. 01243 785421).

## Treyford Hill
*Map 1 ref C5*

*10 miles NW of Chichester off the B2141*

On Treyford Hill a line of rounded mounds known as the **Devil's Jumps** can be seen. The name is derived from the superstitious habit of attributing unusual features in the landscape to the work of Satan. In fact, the five larger and two smaller mounds are bell-barrows - Bronze Age burial sites containing the remains of dead tribal leaders who, having been cremated, were then interred in pottery urns.

Some two miles southeast of Treyford, just south of the crest of the South Downs escarpment, the B2146 road passes **Uppark**, a splendid late-17th century country mansion now owned by the National Trust. During the 1880s, H G Wells spent several years at Uppark where his mother was employed as a housekeeper The upper floors were almost completely destroyed by fire in 1989 (ironically just as a programme of restoration was nearing completion), the biggest restoration programme in the history of the National Trust saw it open again in 1995. Remarkably, most of the largely 18th century contents had been saved and put into safe storage. A testament to the restorers' skill, this fine  house is always busy, and pre-booking is advisable. The gardens, landscaped in the early 19th century by Humphry Repton, feature a woodland walk and afford fine views towards the Solent.

### Compton
Map 1 ref B6

*8 miles NW of Chichester off the B2146*

This tranquil settlement of brick and flint buildings including a church, shop and pub, is handy for nearby Telegraph Hill, atop which stands an exceptional Neolithic long barrow known as **Bevis' Thumb**. This mysterious burial site was named by more recent inhabitants of the area after the legendary giant, Bevis, who, according to folklore, crossed the Solent from the Isle of Wight in a single stride and whose weekly diet consisted of an ox washed down with two hogsheads (150 gallons) of beer.

### The Mardens
Map 1 ref B6

*8 miles NW of Chichester between the B2141 and B2146*

The quiet lanes crisscrossing this section of the west Downs connect four settlements: **North Marden**, **East Marden**, **West Marden** and **Up Marden**. North Marden's church of St Mary is one of the smallest in Sussex, having only a nave and apse. St Michael's at Up Marden stands on the ancient Pilgrims' Way between Winchester and Chichester. Approached through a farmyard, this remotest of churches possesses a delightfully simple 13thcentury interior. From East Marden there is a lovely circular walk through the Forestry Commission's **Wildham Wood**, one of the finest areas of beech and broad-leaved woodlands in the region.

Whilst exploring this area why not visit **Stansted Park** (2 miles SW of West Marden off the B2146). Home of the Earl and Countess of Bessborough, this fine stately manse is surrounded by glorious parkland and enjoys panoramic views down to the English Channel.

### Chilgrove
Map 1 ref C6

*7 miles NW of Chichester off the B2141*

Nestling beneath the South Downs in scenic Chilgrove, on the B2141 between Chichester and Petersfield, **Crows Hall** bed and breakfast is a beautifully evocative 16th century farmhouse occupying a picturesque setting on a quiet country road. Inside you'll find flagstone floors and oak-beamed ceilings, along with all the charm and homeliness that the words '16th century farmhouse' bring to mind. Accommodations are located in a special wing with its own entrance, and both available double rooms are cosy and comfortable. Breakfast - including, if you wish, fresh eggs from the B&B's own freerange hens - is served in the flagstoned back kitchen, which features a wood-burning stove. Weather permitting, you might prefer to take your meal outside in the flower filled walled garden. As the

**Crows Hall Farm**

farmhouse is part of a working 700 acre arable farm, farm walks can be arranged; from the highest point on the farm there are lovely views down to the sea. Scenic walks across the Kingley Vale Nature Reserve and the South Downs begin right from the doorstep. *Crows Hall Farm, Chilgrove, Chichester, West Sussex PO18 9HP Tel: 01243 527855 Fax: 01243 530317*

A pleasant walk to the south of here leads up onto **Bow Hill**, the site of the Iron Age hill fort known as Goosehill Camp whose ancient ramparts can still be made out in the form of two raised earthwork circles.

A couple of miles to the southwest, the B2141 Petersfield to Chichester road passes along the eastern edge of **Kingley Vale National Nature Reserve**. This unique 350 acre forest lies in a shallow valley on the southern slopes of Bow Hill and is Europe's largest yew forest, containing some of the oldest examples of the species in Europe. It is a dark and evocative place, where trees have collapsed and then continued to grow from their horizontal positions, creating a strange series of shapes and forms. Some examples growing on the valley floor are believed to be over 500 years old and have a girth of up to 16 feet. The younger trees - a mere 50 to 100 years old - have seeded themselves on the higher slopes, creating a wonderful mile and a half long nature trail through dark and densely packed woodland circling the site. The forest's origins are a mystery, though it is believed the original trees were valued for making longbows and arrows; because of their military significance, the trees remained under royal protection until the reign of Elizabeth I. Towards the summit of Bow Hill, the trees give way to heather and open heathland; here, a group of four Bronze Age burial mounds (two bell

*11*

and two bowl-barrows) can be found which together are known as the King's Graves or Devil's Humps. The view from the summit extends to Chichester Harbour.

### Stoughton

*Map 1 ref B6*

*5 miles NW of Chichester off the B2141*

Tucked away in the heart of the Sussex Downs between Chilgrove and Emsworth in the village of Stoughton, *The Hare & Hounds* pub dates back 300 years to the reign of William and Mary. The massive sash windows of this beautiful flint built country pub overlook lovely front and back gardens, each offering stunning views. The back garden is particularly lovely, filled with hanging baskets of flowers and a spreading acacia tree. Inside, open log fires and the original oak-beamed ceilings add to the warm ambience provided by owners Peter and Kathy Campbell. A family run business for 20

**The Hare & Hounds**

years, the pub is a Free House offering real ales and superb home-prepared and home-cooked meals. The choice of meals is excellent, with fresh fish and game among the specialities. The Campbells and their staff offer you a friendly welcome that matches the cosy, relaxing and very comfortable surroundings. No booking is necessary and children are made welcome. *Hare & Hounds, Stoughton, Near Chichester, West Sussex PO18 9JP  Tel: 01705 631433*

## Singleton
Map 1 ref C6

*7 miles N of Chichester, off the A286*

Singleton is an attractive community of handsome flint and brick buildings standing on the old Chichester to London road in the valley of the River Lavant. Prior to the Norman invasion, the local manor, one of the largest and wealthiest in England, was owned by Earl Godwin of Wessex, father of the ill-fated King Harold. The village church of St Mary's was built in the 13th century on the foundations of a Saxon predecessor. Inside there are a number of interesting monuments, including two Purbeck marble edifices erected in memory of two successive Earls of Arundel who died within two years of each other in the mid-1500s. Singleton also possesses two fine inns and a characteristic village green with a cricket pitch whose pavilion, an ancient Sussex barn, was moved to its present position from a nearby field.

Singleton is also the home of the famous **Weald and Downland Open Air Museum**, an exemplary museum with reconstructed vernacular rural buildings from all over Kent and Sussex - including a Titchfield's former Tudor market hall, tollhouse, an 18 century granary a working blacksmith's forge and watermill, a Victorian schoolroom and farmhouse and agricultural buildings from the 15th and 16th centuries. This fascinating and unusual collection is situated in a delightful 40 acre parkland setting on the southern edge of the village. Founded in 1971 by J R Armstrong, the museum's structures were all at one time under threat of demolition, before being transported here. The museum also arranges special demonstrations of rural skills, such as thatching, shearing and charcoal burning. There is also a lovely woodland nature trail and picnic area beside the millpond.

## West Dean
Map 1 ref C6

*5 miles N of Chichester off the A286*

The beautiful 35 acre **West Dean Gardens** contain old rose species, a 100 yard pergola, wild garden, walled kitchen garden and a fine collection of rare trees, shrubs and stately mature conifers in St Roche's Arboretum and Park. Visitors can enjoy the two mile circular stroll taking in many of the Gardens treasures. There is also an interesting exhibition of antique lawn mowers dating from 1850, including pony powered mowers and early mechanically driven garden machinery.

A good place to stop on your journeys is **The Selsey Arms**, a handsome and welcoming Free House on the main road in the village of West Dean. Originally a much smaller Tudor building, it now incorporates the once derelict, now carefully restored former village hall next door. The pretty, whitewashed stone and clapboard exterior is trimmed with hanging baskets of flowers. A colourful and informative collection of race cards adorns the surround of the public bar - on loan from a local jockey, a reminder of the area's connections with Goodwood. The dining area is intimate and cheerful. Apart from the traditional bar snacks, chef Richard is a master at staples such as home-made steak and kidney pie and more ad-

**The Selsey Arms**

venturous cuisine such as broccoli and potato in cream cheese sauce, farmhouse pate and toast, sweet and sour chicken stir fry, the unusual and delicious wheat casserole and a selection of fresh seafood dishes - all home-prepared and home-cooked. Owners Michael and Margaret Hayes and their sons take great pride in and work very hard to achieve the standard of service on offer, and it shows. *The Selsey Arms, West Dean, Near Chichester, West Sussex PO18 0QX Tel: 01243 811246*

A mile or so to the south of West Dean, the land rises towards the ancient hilltop site known as **The Trundle**, one of the four main Neolithic settlements in the county. The 12 acre site was later fortified during the Iron Age between 300 and 100 BC when massive circular earthwork ramparts and a dry ditch were constructed. The hill fort has two entrances, arranged in such a way as to expose attackers to defensive fire from above. Named after the Old English word for wheel, the Trundle enjoys fine views over Chichester, Singleton and nearby Goodwood Racecourse.

Close by the Coach House is a relaxing bed and breakfast hotel located in the medieval village of Binderton, mentioned in the Domesday Book (in which it was assessed at roughly 300 acres in area). Once, as its name suggests, the coach house of 17th century Binderton House, next door (when the population of Binderton - 19 adults in 1641 - was barely more than the occupants of Binderton House itself), this handsome B & B is situated amid lovely gardens set back from the main road. Close to West Dean College, Goodwood race-

*The Coach House*

course and the coast, with many golf courses in the area and affording excellent walks and lovely views over the surrounding countryside, this supremely comfortable B & B offers two tastefully furnished and spacious self-contained apartments. Proprietor Sandra Pightling makes guests most welcome and is happy to pass on her knowledge of local sites of natural beauty and historical interest: as mentioned, Binderton House has long been of particular importance in the locality, and was also in more recent times the home of Sir Anthony Eden. *The Coach House, Binderton, Near Chichester PO18 0JS Tel: 01243 539624*

## The Lavants
Map 1 ref C7

*3 miles N of Chichester off the A286*

Mid Lavant and East Lavant are two attractive villages which are named after the small river which flows southwards from Singleton to Chichester Harbour. The church of St Nicholas in Mid Lavant contains an interesting 17th century monument to Lady Mary May, by the sculptor John Bushnell. The spectacular view from here across the Downs is said to be the inspiration for those immortal words *'England's Green and Pleasant Land'* which appear in William Blake's famous poem, *Jerusalem*.

While you are visiting the beautiful Lavants, there is a superb choice of places to stay. Originally two farm cottages now converted into a charming and cosy bed and breakfast hotel, **Rose Cottage** in East Lavant is approached down a narrow country lane, surrounded by lush greenery. The brick and flint exterior adds to the rustic ambience; inside, guests will find every home comfort. The two guest rooms are decorated with great care and taste, in keeping with the

**Rose Cottage**

attention and solicitude brought by owners Nicola and Charles Burton to every area of their guests' welfare. This is a family run establishment, and guests are made to feel as special and welcome as one of the family. There are lovely scenic walks that begin right on the doorstep, and guests also have use of the small patio area, a sun-trap all year round. Visitors are known to return again and again for the tranquillity and warm welcome they know they will find at this lovely B&B in the peaceful and picturesque heart of Sussex. It's a good idea to book well in advance. *Rose Cottage, Shop Lane, East Lavant, nr Chichester, West Sussex PO18 0BA Tel: 01243 787659*

**The Flint House** - so called because of its original 17th century flint-built exterior - is also set in the captivating village of East Lavant. Approached down a quiet country lane, through rustic gates and along an impressive forecourt lined with towering trees, this delightful bed and breakfast offers self-contained accommodations in an extension to the original buildings. Proprietor Mrs Vivien Read

*The Flint House*

offers her guests a warm welcome in superior surroundings; the furnishings and fittings are of the highest quality and assure every comfort and convenience. A separate entrance for guests means that they can come and go as they please, and there is excellent walking and bird watching right on the doorstep. The extensive gardens are a haven of tranquil repose. Also within walking distance of Goodwood Golf Course and Aero Club, this B&B makes a perfect base for exploring the delights of nearby Goodwood House and the attractive towns of Petworth, Midhurst, Chichester and Bognor Regis, as well as the surrounding Sussex countryside and many incomparable hamlets and villages in the area. *The Flint House, Pook Lane, East Lavant, Chichester, West Sussex PO18 0AS Tel: 01243 773482*

## Halnaker
Map 1 ref D7

*4 miles NE of Chichester off the A285*

The village of Halnaker (pronounced Hannacker) was the seat of the influential and powerful De La Warr family. It contains a fine modern country residence, **Halnaker House**, which was designed by Edwin Lutyens in 1938. An earlier Halnaker House was built in mediaeval times by the De Haye family, founders of Boxgrove Priory; situated to the north of its modern counterpart, it fell into ruin around 1800. Above the village on Halnaker Hill stands an early 18th century tower **windmill** which remained in use until 1905. The exterior was restored in 1934, enabling the structure to used as an observation tower during the Second World War; the internal workings, however, have been removed. Hilaire Belloc wrote a famous poem about Halnaker Windmill in 1912 when it was still in ruins.

## Goodwood
Map 1 ref D7

*4 miles N of Chichester off the A285*

One of the reasons the original Halnaker House was allowed to decay was that it was overshadowed by **Goodwood House**, the spectacular country home a mile and a half northwest of Halnaker village. Acquired by the first Duke of Richmond in 1697 so that he could ride with the local hunt, it started out as a rather unexceptional brick residence, but was rebuilt on a grand scale in the late 18th century for the third Duke of Richmond by the architect James Wyatt, at which time the grand stables were added.

Several rooms in this impressive house, including the state apartments, are now open to visitors; items on show include paintings by Canaletto and Stubbs, fine Sevres porcelain, some gruesome relics from the Napoleonic Wars, an assortment of royal gifts and many fine pieces of English and French furniture.

Goodwood House is the focal point of the **Goodwood Estate**, 12,000 acres of downland which incorporate the home of the famous 'Glorious Goodwood' horse racing meeting each July - as well as approximately 18 other racedays a year and a monthly antiques market - a 60 acre country park, a superb motor racing circuit, golf course, airfield and children's adventure play area.

## Tangmere
Map 1 ref D7

*3 miles E of Chichester off the A27*

At Tangmere Airfield, based around the former RAF base where H E Bates completed his novel, *Fair Stood the Wind for France*, there is an interesting museum dedicated to Britain's military flying personnel. ***The Tangmere Military Aviation Museum*** tells the story - with replica aircraft, photographs, pictures, models and memorabilia - of military flying from the earliest days to the present time. Exhibits include uniform displays, RAF regiments' armaments and Desert Air Force models; in the Battle of Britain hall, aircraft remains, personal effects, photographs and paintings, both British and German, pay tribute to the air war over southern England from 1939 to 1945. In the Merston Hall, built in the style of a hangar, can be found two actual historical aircraft, each of which beat the World Speed Records in their day. These magnificent machines, on loan from the RAF, are a tribute to

*the Tangmere Military Aviation Museum*

Tangmere itself, as both speed records were made from here. Open daily March to October 10-5.30; February and November 10-4.30; last admission one hour before closing. Admission charge. Free parking, souvenir shop, cafeteria, picnic area, memorial garden. Access for the disabled. *Tangmere Military Aviation Museum Trust, Tangmere, Near Chichester, West Sussex PO20 6ES   Tel: 01243 775223.*

## Boxgrove
*Map 1 ref D7*

*3 miles NE of Chichester off the A27*

**Boxgrove Priory** lies on the opposite side of the A27, a mile to the north of Tangmere. Now a collection of monastic buildings and other ruins surrounding the still complete parish church of St Mary and St Blaise, this once glorious Benedictine priory began life around 1115 as an outpost of Lessay Abbey in France. The parish church is itself one of the most outstanding Early English churches in the region. Initially a community of only three monks, over the centuries Boxgrove grew to become one of the most influential monastic houses in Sussex.

The sumptuous interior of the sturdily built great church reflects the institution's former importance; the roof is supported by Purbeck marble columns and there is a wonderful series of 15th century ceiling paintings by Lambert Barnard, and a marvellous free standing chantry.

Perhaps most lavish, however, is the De La Warr Chantry Chapel, a miniature 'church within a church' which was built by the local lord of the manor as a proposed resting place for himself and his wife. His plans, however, were upset by Henry VIII's Dissolution of the Monasteries, and despite taking ownership of the priory for a time, he was subsequently forced to dispose of this wonderful building. De La Warr was eventually buried at Broadwater, near Worthing, the extravagant marble chapel at Boxgrove remaining empty.

Elsewhere in the village, the 17th century **Nightingale Cottages** and 18th century **Derby Almshouses** are worth making the effort to find.

A fascinating discovery was recently made by local archaeologists, who unearthed the prehistoric bones of what is thought to be one of the world's oldest human beings. Scientists are still debating the precise age of *'Boxgrove Man'*.

## Fishbourne                                              *Map 1 ref C8*
*2 miles W of Chichester off the A27*

Fishbourne marks the site of the largest non-military Roman building yet to be uncovered in Britain. **Fishbourne Roman Palace** was only rediscovered in 1960 when a new water main was being laid for a proposed housing scheme.

The work revealed the remains of a grand and luxuriously fitted Roman villa set around a 250 foot square courtyard. This magnificent villa with its 100 odd rooms was occupied from the 1st to the 3rd centuries AD. It is believed to have been built between 75 and 100 AD for King Cogidubnus of the Atrebates, a leader of the ancient Britons who co-operated with the Romans and took on the role of Viceroy. His reward for collaborating was a palace containing an underfloor heating system, hot baths, a colonnade, an ornamental courtyard garden, and a series of elaborate floor mosaics, wall paintings and Purbeck marble carvings. The building is thought to have been largely destroyed by fire around 320 AD and then abandoned.

Present day visitors to Fishbourne can see the layout of the Roman Palace, including sections of the walls, plumbing and heating systems. They can also admire the remains of some 25 superb floor mosaics (the largest collection in Europe), the most outstanding of which is a 17 foot square panel with a central medallion depicting the winged Cupid sitting astride a dolphin. A recently constructed building protects the remains of the north wing allowing visitors to view the original rooms and corridors from above. There is also an interesting museum on the site describing the history of the palace and its role in the local economy of the day, along with a reconstruction of a 2nd century dining room, a garden laid out according to its 1st century plan, and an informative audio-visual presentation.

## East Ashling
*Map 1 ref C7*
*2 miles NW of Chichester off the B2178*

Quite near Fishbourne, as well as Chichester, the coast and scenic countryside, the village of East Ashling, situated in a conservation area designated as being of 'outstanding natural beauty', is home to **Englewood**, a comfortable and cosy B&B offering a quiet, convenient base for touring in the area - within a few minutes' walk of views of the Downs. Sylvia Jones is the B&B's charming and helpful owner, with a wide-ranging knowledge of local history and su-

***Englewood***

perb culinary skills. She takes great pride in catering for the individual needs and tastes of her guests - as the B&B offers just two double rooms, personalised service is guaranteed. All meals are freshly prepared and home-cooked, using local ingredients wherever possible. The extensive evening meal menu includes traditional fare such as home-made meat pies and an excellent range of fresh fish dishes, including scampi, prawns and salmon. Packed lunches are also available on request, and Mrs Jones will fill your thermos with tea or coffee free of charge. Guests' also have use of their own private entrance. *Englewood, Main Road, East Ashling, West Sussex PO18 9AS Tel: 01243 575407*

## Bosham

*Map 1 ref B8*

*3 miles SW of Chichester off the A27*

A couple of miles to the southwest of Fishbourne, the idyllic village of Bosham (pronounced Boz-am) stands beside Chichester Harbour on its own small peninsula. An important settlement since the days of the Romans, the Irish monk Dicul established a church here in the 7th century on the foundations of a Roman basilica, predating

***Bosham Quay***

St Wilfrid's community at Selsey by several years. The village has strong associations with King Canute, whose youngest daughter is thought to have been buried here in the 11th century. (Indeed, a stone coffin containing a child's skeleton was discovered in the floor of the church in 1865). Bosham's Quay Meadow may even have been the site of Canute's infamous confrontation with nature when the dauntless monarch, believing his power and influence to be absolute, ordered the incoming tide to roll back (predictably, he and his courtiers got very wet indeed).

Quay Meadow features again a few decades later when King

Harold embarked here in 1064 on his abortive journey to appease his rival for the English crown, William, Duke of Normandy. However, Harold's plans went awry when he was taken captive and made to swear to assist William in his claim to the throne, a promise which Harold failed to keep. This forced William into making a return visit and a couple of years later, he landed on the beaches near Hastings with decidedly more successful results. (Harold's Sussex estates were among the first to be seized by the conquering Normans.) Bosham's characteristic Saxon church spire, one of the finest of its kind in the country, is featured alongside Harold's ship on the Bayeux Tapestry.

In more recent times, the painter Rex Whistler was a resident at the Old Ship in 1944, at which time it was an exclusive club. On one of the walls he painted his last work, just two days before meeting his death on the beaches of Normandy.

***The Berkeley Arms*** is a handsome brick-built public house located close to the sea, here in the picturesque village of Bosham, popular for walking, fishing and sailing. Angela Shields and Andrew Hayes cater for all their diverse visitors, providing an excellent range of beers and wines, including a selection of very potent home-brewed vintages, as well as delicious set meals and bar snacks, all served in generous portions. The atmosphere in this impressive establishment is cosy and relaxed, with open fireplaces, wooden tables and impressive old black and white photographs of the surrounding region adorning the walls. Visitors are encouraged to add their own homespun philosophical comments to those etched in chalk on the exposed ceiling beams. The hospitality and pleasant surroundings of this wonderful es-

***The Berkeley Arms***

tablishment are hard to beat, making it the perfect place for a quiet drink and other refreshment, in a location that is convenient for all local attractions. *The Berkeley Arms, Bosham Lane, Bosham, West Sussex PO18 8HG Tel: 01243 573167.*

The Bosham of today is a must for those keen on yachting, birdwatching or just relaxing in delightful surroundings. The streets are filled with elegant 17th and 18th century flint and redbrick shops, pubs and residential buildings, those on the sea front having short flights of steps to prevent the occasional invasion of the sea through the front door. An interesting place to visit is the Bosham Walk craft centre and art gallery in Bosham Lane - but be warned: visitors are often tempted to park beside the harbour side road, only to discover their car half-submerged when they return some hours later at high tide.

## Chidham                                      *Map 1 ref B8*
*5 miles W of Chichester off the A27*

Just two miles west of Bosham, overlooking Chichester Harbour, the charming **Easton House** bed and breakfast hotel is located in a romantic ivy covered 17th century country house set in lush gardens and overlooking adjacent farmland and the sea - the ideal location for scenic walks, bird watching and touring in the area. There is nothing pretentious about this cosy and comfortable hotel; owner Mary Hartley anticipates her guests' every need and greets them with tea and a warm welcome in the guests' sitting room. The two guest bedrooms are decorated in traditional style, furnished with antiques and ornaments collected by Mrs Hartley. The oak beams

**Easton House**

and stone-clad floors add to the period atmosphere of this peaceful and welcoming establishment. Mrs Hartley holds occasional chamber music evenings for the pleasure and entertainment of her guests - and guests are welcome to tickle the ivories of the marvellous Bechstein piano. Graceful, over-arching walnut and magnolia trees line the paths in the secluded rear garden, a lovely spot for an afternoon or evening of total relaxation. *Easton House, Chidham Lane, Chidham, West Sussex PO18 8TF  Tel: 01243 572514*

### Apuldram                                            Map 1 ref C8
*2 miles SW of Chichester off the A286*
Apuldram is an attractive village on the Chichester Channel with a number of fascinating places to visit. It has a lovely 13th century church down by the harbour near several waterside pubs. The 15th century manor house, **Rymans**, is very handsome. Apuldram Roses, a specialist rose nursery, is particularly spectacular in summer.

### Birdham                                             Map 1 ref C8
*4 miles SW of Chichester off the A286*
Birdham is the setting for Turner's famous painting of Chichester Harbour which is now on view at Petworth House. The village also has a 16th century parish church with an unusually small door which, according to local legend, was partially blocked to prevent Satan from returning after he had been forcibly thrown out. This pretty village is also home to the **Sussex Falconry Centre** (approached through Locsacre Aquatic Nursery, Wophams Lane), orginally set up as a breeding and rescue centre, now open to the public, where can be seen falcons, hawks, owls and eagles. At nearby Itchenor, waterborne tours of Chichester Harbour are available throughout the year.

### West Wittering                                      Map 1 ref B9
*7 miles SW of Chichester off the B2179*
The charming seaside village of West Wittering stands at the western tip of the Selsey peninsula, close to the narrow entrance to Chichester Harbour. This former fishing village has been carefully developed as a small and select residential community and holiday resort. There are excellent sandy beaches here, along with some noteworthy buildings, including the parish church of St Peter and St Paul, and **Cakeham Manor House** with its distinctive early 16th century brick tower. This splendid part-mediaeval, part-Tudor, part-Georgian country residence was originally built as a summer palace for the bishops of Chichester.

The sandy stretch of land jutting out into the eastern approaches to Chichester Harbour is known as **East Head**. Now under the ownership of the National Trust, this 110 acre sand and shingle spit supports a variety of bird, plant and marine life. In recent years, marram grass has been introduced to the sand dunes to reduce the ravages of the sea, wind and visitors' footsteps. A walk around the headland is well worth doing and takes about an hour.

### Earnley

*Map 1 ref B9*

*5 miles SW of Chichester off the B2198*

This charming small village has an interesting 14th century church. Earnley Gardens is a 5 acre site with 17 themed gardens, exotic birds and butterflies, as well as a a museum of military vehicles, a small animal farm, and 'Rejectamenta' - an unusual museum describing itself as a 'nostalgia centre', with thousands of everyday items on display reflecting the changes in lifestyle which have occurred over the past 100 years.

### Selsey

*Map 1 ref C9*

*7 miles S of Chichester off the B2145*

Selsey Bill, the southeastern tip of the Selsey peninsula, is the southernmost point in Sussex; from here there are some fine views along the coast and across to the Isle of Wight. Over the centuries this part of the coastline has been gradually eroded and many of the area's most important historic remains have been lost beneath the encroaching tides. The popular resort of Selsey lies to the north and east. There is an interesting **Lifeboat Museum** here at Selsey Lifeboat Station.

If you choose to stay in the area, **St Andrews Lodge** on the Manhood Peninsula in Selsey, 7 miles south of Chichester and only

**St Andrews Lodge**

a short distance from the sea, is a welcoming and homely family run bed and breakfast hotel offering a friendly, relaxed atmosphere in an excellent location for exploring Chichester, Arundel, Portsmouth and the West Sussex coast. Proprietor Mrs Valma Kennedy brings style and a wealth of experience to the preparation and cooking of her farmhouse style breakfasts; evening meals are also available on request. The hotel is accessible to wheelchairs, offering ground floor bedrooms and an entrance ramp. The roomy, attractive public lounge has floor to ceiling french windows at one end overlooking the lovely, sun-filled garden, where guests are invited to make use of the sun chairs and loungers. Guests can also take advantage of the nearby golf, fishing, horse-riding and watersports facilities, and then relax in the residents-only licensed bar. Ample private parking also available. *St Andrews Lodge, Chichester Road, Selsey, Chichester, West Sussex PO20 0LX Tel/Fax: 01243 606899*

In the 1860s the decision was made to move the medieval parish church of St Peter to Selsey from its lonely position at Church Norton, one and a half miles to the north. According to ecclesiastical law, however, a church chancel cannot be moved, and so this remains in its original location as a chapel. St Wilfrid founded a monastery near Selsey which subsequently became a cathedral; however, in the 11th century the Normans relocated the centre of the diocese to Chichester and the original cathedral site was left to the mercy of the encroaching waves; it now lies some distance offshore.

St Wilfrid's chapel at **Church Norton** stands beside the remains of a Norman motte and bailey castle on the edge of **Pagham Harbour** and is well worth a visit. Pagham's stone-built parish chuch dedicated to St Thomas a Becket and was probably built within a few years of the Saint's murder at Canterbury in 1170. Barton Manor is reputedly the oldest continuously occupied manor house in Britain; thought to be over 1,200 years old, it has its own chapel and was part of the property given to Bishop Wilfred by King Ethewald of the West Saxons in AD 683.

## Sidlesham
Map 1 ref C9
*4 miles S of Chichester off the B2145*

The pleasant community of Sidlesham is home to an interesting information and interpretation centre for the 1,000 acre **Pagham Harbour** which is managed by the West Sussex County Council as a nature reserve. Its tidal mud flats attract an abundance of animal and marine life and the site is an important breeding ground for a number of bird species, including the little tern. Sidlesham Ferry is also the starting point for guided walks around this important conservation area.

The picturesque ***Crab & Lobster*** public house occupies a quiet country lane in this lovely village. Dating back to the 1600s, this country pub is a welcoming haven of tranquillity with real character and real oak beamed ceilings. The ambience is friendly and inviting, as owners Brian and Liz Cross have a knack for making every visitor feel special. Brian brings the benefit of his 37 years of experience to bear on maintaining just the right atmosphere of warmth

*Crab & Lobster*

and bonhomie. There are lovely and well tended gardens to the rear, and two bars in which to enjoy a drink and a meal. As a Free House, the choices of what to drink include any one of four real ales. All the food is home-cooked and home-prepared; dishes range from steaks, fresh haddock and cumberland pie to balti dishes, cantonese prawns - and, of course, crab and lobster. *The Crab & Lobster, Mill Lane, Sidlesham, Chichester, West Sussex PO20 7NB  Tel: 01243 641233*

### Hunston                                        Map 1 ref C8
*2 miles S of Chichester off the B2145*

Located in this quiet rural village just on the outskirts of Chichester, ***Hunston Mill*** offers several different types of self-catering accommodation. A working mill until the early 1900s, and dating back in parts to the 1500s, the mill and its buildings were purchased in the 1850s by one James Hodson, a churchwarden who also played cricket for Sussex. A coach house and stable were added in 1891, and these two fine buildings have been converted to holiday homes sleeping up to five people each. The mill tower has been restored and contains two delightful flats which sleep two people each; the Engine House, which once powered the mill, is now also a holiday home for two. Owners Tricia and Richard Beeny take pride in affording their guests every convenience - including the daily papers

**Hunston Mill**

free upon request. There is also a laundry area for guests. The extensive garden takes up nearly an acre and affords serene views over the South Downs. It has lawns for croquet and other games, the Summerhouse for a quiet rest, and a barbecue in what remains of the old Mill Cottage. *Hunston Mill, Hunston, Chichester, West Sussex PO20 6AU  Tel: 01243 783375  Fax: 01243 785179*

## Bognor Regis to Shoreham-by-Sea

### *Bognor Regis*                                      Map 1 ref D9
*5 miles SE of Chichester off the A259*
At the end of the 18th century, Bognor was transformed from a quiet fishing village by Sir Richard Hotham, a wealthy London milliner who had ambitions of creating a rival for Brighton, Eastbourne and Bournemouth. He set about constructing some imposing residences, including the Dome in Upper Bognor Road, and even planned to have his creation renamed Hothampton.

However, the fashionable set of the day stayed away in droves, and Hotham's dream was never realised - at least not until 1929, when George V convalesced in the town following a serious illness. On the strength of this royal patronage, Bognor was granted the title Regis (of the King).

Today, Bognor Regis is a pleasant south coast resort town with some elegant Regency features, traditional public gardens, a children's fun park, a lovely long, sandy beach, a pier and a 'subtropical waterworld' at Butlin's South Coast World.

The resort hosts the annual Birdman Rally, usually held in August. This competition involves a variety of winged contestants launching themselves off the pier in an attempt to make the longest unpowered flight. There is also an informative local history museum at **Hotham Park Lodge** in the High Street.

### Felpham
*1 mile E of Bognor off the A259*                                              *Map 1 ref E8*

Located on the eastern side of Bognor, the village of Felpham is a pleasant sailing centre with a lovely church. The artist and writer William Blake lived here between 1800 and 1803, and in describing the location wrote 'Heaven opens here on all sides her golden gates.'

**The Garden Room** in Felpham is somewhere to consider if you are thinking of staying in the area. In this former granary annexe now converted into two self contained ground floor apartments, guests can choose between self-catering or bed and breakfast accommodation. Located just 100 yards from the sandy beach at Felpham and within easy distance of Chichester, Portsmouth and other local places of interest, this comfortable and picturesque establishment offers year-round accommodation in a tranquil suburb

**The Garden Room**

of Bognor Regis. Owners Sue and Roger Harden make every effort to make your stay relaxing, including the offer of a baby-sitting service if required. Each of the rooms is tastefully furnished and overlooks a small, secluded garden, which gives this delightful B&B its name. Accommodations comprise The Rose Room, large enough for two to four persons and including a fully-equipped kitchen, and The Green Room, a luxurious double room with adjoining breakfast nook. Evening meals are also provided on request, or guests may choose from one of the several restaurants and public houses within walking distance. *The Garden Room, 12 Brigham Place, Felpham, Bognor Regis, West Sussex PO22 7NW  Tel: 01243 586379*

## Yapton
Map 1 ref E8

*2 miles NE of Bognor off the B2233*

**The Maypole Inn** in Yapton is a handsome whitewashed stone-built public house offering cool beers, real ales and home-cooked food. Situated down a quiet country lane, this Free House upholds the finest traditions of the English country inn: the ambience is

welcoming and the decor, complete with wood-beamed ceilings, pine tongue and groove panelling and oak tables and chairs, cosy and very comfortable.. During the winter there are log fires in the public bar and the saloon bar; the public bar is lively, the saloon bar peaceful and relaxing. On the premises there's also a very popular skittle alley, which is separate from, but has ready access to, the public and saloon bars, and which can be booked. A selection of real ales from the main and independent brewer-

*The Maypole Inn*

ies, as well as lagers and ciders, are available — the skittle alley has its own bar serving two real ales; up to six others are available in the other bars. Proprietors Keith and Jennifer McManus also offer great food, including traditional hearty favourites such as steak and mushroom pie. *The Maypole Inn, Maypole Lane, Yapton, West Sussex BN18 0DP Tel: 01243 551417.*

## Littlehampton
*Map 2 ref F8*

*5 miles E of Bognor off the A259*

At the mouth of the River Arun, Littlehampton is a pleasant coastal town which has all the ingredients for a traditional seaside holiday. As well as safe sandy beaches and a harbour, there is a promenade, a funfair, a swimming and sports centre, a boating lake, an amusement park, a cinema, a theatre, and an 18 hole golf course on the western side of the river; Littlehampton is also a popular yachting centre and pleasure boat trips are available for trips up the river to Arundel and Amberley.

Despite appearing to have been specially made for holidaymakers, the modern face of Littlehampton only developed after 1860 when the railway first connected it with London. Prior to that, the town had a rich past and was an important port for several hundreds of years up until the 1500s. Signs of Roman occupation have been discovered here, and the local manor is mentioned in the Domesday Book. After the Norman Invasion, Littlehampton became an important cross-Channel port, importing stone from Caen and exporting timber from the Sussex Weald. In 1139, Queen Matilda landed here from France to launch her abortive campaign to claim the English throne from her cousin, Stephen.

Further information on the history of the town can be found at the informative **Littlehampton Museum** which is located in the old Manor House in Church Street. Another interesting museum, **The Rustington Heritage Centre**, details the social and cultural history of the district; it is situated in the parish council offices in **Rustington**, the town bordering Littlehampton to the east. To the west, beyond the River Arun, there's an extensive region of unspoilt dunes. Rustington's church of St Peter and St Paul has a 12th century tower,

## Lyminster
*Map 2 ref F8*

*2 miles N of Littlehampton off the A284*

Lyminster is an ancient settlement of flint-built cottages and protective walls which appears (as Lullyngminster) in Alfred the Great's will of 901. A marvellous view of Arundel Castle can be enjoyed from here, this time looking northwest across the water meadows of the lower Arun. Local legend has it that the deep pool known as the Knucker Hole, which lies 100 yards northwest of Lyminster church, was once inhabited by a savage sea dragon. This monster was said to have terrorised the local population to such an extent that the King of Wessex offered half his kingdom and his daughter's hand in marriage to the man who killed the beast. The dragon was finally done away with after a terrible fight, either by a gallant young farm boy known as Jim Pulk, or by a handsome knight, depending on which version of the legend you choose to read. Both versions agree, however, that the ancient tombstone in the north transept of the church is where the conquering hero was finally laid to rest - it is still known today as the Slayer's Stone.

## Poling
Map 2 ref F8

*2 miles NE of Littlehampton off the A280*

Poling was once the regional headquarters of the Knights Hospitallers. This holy order of the Hospital of St John of Jerusalem (a present day descendant of which is the St John's Ambulance Brigade) was founded around 1070 as a sanctuary for Christian travellers making the pilgrimage to the Holy Land. However, during the Crusades the order took on a more military role and became hugely wealthy as a result of some clever manoeuvring; they later established themselves throughout the eastern Mediterranean and then across the whole of western Europe. The Knights founded an important preceptory in Poling, and some of its remains, including the chapel, now form part of a private residence which still goes by the name of *St John's Priory*.

## Ferring
Map 2 ref G8

*5 miles E of Littlehampton off the A27*

Ferring, and the nearby coastal communities of *East Preston*, *Angmering-on-Sea* and *Goring-by-Sea*, have a pleasant suburban air much loved by those in search of a peaceful retirement or holiday. The towns grew rapidly from small fishing villages following the arrival of the railways in the mid-19th century. An impressive avenue of mature ilex oaks connects Ferring with Goring-by-Sea, and the *English Martyrs Catholic Church* in Goring contains an astonishing replica of Michelangelo's Sistine Chapel ceiling, approximately two-thirds the size of the original, completed in 1992 by local craftsman, Gary Bevans. Other relics from the past include *St Mary's church* in East Preston, *St Andrew's* in Ferring, a neat little early English church full of tablets to the Henty and Olliver families, and a sprinkling of old cottages dating from pre-Victorian times. Modern Angmering-on-Sea has a couple of good restaurants and hotels, and East Preston a locally renowned eating place, the Old Forge Restaurant.

***The Henty Arms***

Built around 1830, some seven years before the young Queen Victoria took the throne, ***The Henty Arms*** has long played a central role in the picturesque village of Ferring. Henty was the name of prominent local landowners; now owned by Vernon and Carol Carlyle, this fine public house has been since its inception the social hub of this small village community; it maintains this role today with its two football teams, cricket team and pool and darts teams, and keeps to its family and community orientated roots by extending a warm welcome to all visitors. Spacious and comfortable, this handsome establishment offers great home-prepared and home-cooked food as well as excellent beers and ales. Situated just 1 mile from Worthing and within a short distance of interesting shops, the sea, country walks, stately homes, Goodwood races and the polo grounds, it makes an ideal stopover point; there is also one room available to guests who would like to spend a bit more time in this lovely part of West Sussex. *The Henty Arms, 2 Ferring Lane, Ferring, Near Worthing, West Sussex BN12 6QY Tel: 01903 241254 Fax: 01903 503796*

## Worthing
*Map 2 ref H8*

*8 miles E of Littlehampton off the A259*

Continuing eastwards along the coast, the next port of call is the sizable resort of Worthing. Despite having been inhabited since the stone age, Worthing remained a small and isolated fishing community until the end of the 18th century when the combined effects of a new northern road link through the Findon Gap and the sudden popularity of sea bathing among the rich and fashionable set led to a period of rapid development. This reached its peak after 1798, when George III sent his 16 year old daughter, Princess Amelia, to

Worthing to recuperate from an ill-favoured affair with one of his royal equerries. During this period, several fine Regency thoroughfares were constructed, most notably Warwick Road, Montague Place, Liverpool Terrace and Park Terrace, all of which survive today.

By 1830, however, Worthing's Golden Age had come to an end. Further expansion was interrupted by the cholera and typhoid outbreaks of the 1850s and 1890s, and it was not until the inter-war years of the 20th century that the town once again saw a period of development, albeit of a less grandiose kind. Today, Worthing is a bustling seaside town with a pier, theatre and cinemas which offers some excellent shopping and entertainment facilities in an atmosphere of dignified Regency charm.

Visitors interested in finding out more about the town's history from Neolithic times to the present day should make a point of finding the award-winning **Worthing Museum and Art Gallery** in Chapel Road, which has an extremely rich archeological collection. Other exhibits include a model of a Neolithic flint mine, Anglo-Saxon glass and jewellery, a fascinating collection of antique toys and dolls, and a display of English paintings, glassware and china from the Regency period onwards. There is also a fine sculpture garden.

As Worthing expanded during the 19th century, it swallowed up a number of ancient nearby settlements: **Broadwater** contains some fine old cottages and a Norman church with two ornate carved arches and a number of fine monuments, and **West Tarring** contains the remains of a 13th century palace belonging to the Archbishops of Canterbury, the central building of which now doubles as a village hall and primary school annexe; nearby there's a 250 year old fig garden. West Tarring's High Street features a group of exceptional timber-framed houses dating from the 15th century known as Parsonage Row; restored by the Sussex Archeological Society, the row features an interesting museum of folklore.

### Sompting                                    Map 2 ref H8
*2 miles NE of Worthing off the A27*

The parish church of **St Mary the Virgin** at Sompting was built to a design which is unique in Britain. The distinctive spire consists of four diamond shaped faces which taper to a point; known as a Rhenish helm - the form was popular in Rhineland Germany but is unknown elsewhere in the UK. This largely Saxon structure dates from well before the Norman Conquest; however, in 1154 it was acquired by the Knights Templars who carried out a number of major alterations. Growing unease about the Templars' unbridled power led to their disbandment in 1312; the church then passed into the hands of their great rivals, the Knights Hospitallers, who decided to 'restore' the spire and settled upon the present design, which they considered was in keeping with original Saxon structure.

### North and South Lancing
*2 miles E of Worthing off the A259*

*Map 2 ref H7*

South Lancing is a residential area built to house the workforce of the Lancing railway carriage works, which relocated here in 1910 and continued to operate until the 1960s. By contrast, the most distinctive feature in North Lancing is its famous public school, **Lancing College**, whose lofty chapel stands out above the valley of the River Adur. The school was founded 1848 by Nathaniel Woodard, a

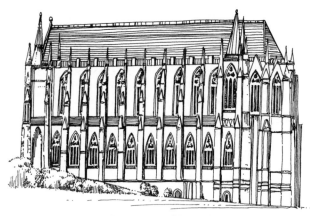

*Lancing Chapel*

curate at nearby New Shoreham whose ambition was to establish a group of 'classless' schools. (By the time of his death in 1891, 15 schools had joined his federation.) Despite its French Gothic style, the great chapel was only completed in recent years; its towering floodlit walls and hilltop location make it a striking feature on the nighttime horizon.

### Coombes
*3 miles NE of Worthing off the A283*

*Map 2 ref H7*

The tiny settlement of Coombes holds only a few houses and a farmyard; the only other building in the hamlet is a modest church, worth taking a closer look at. This unassuming building contains some exceptional 12th century murals of the Nativity, uncovered in 1949 and believed to have been painted by the group from St Pancras Priory, Lewes, who were also responsible for those at Clayton and

Hardham. Coombes churchyard is entered through a rare tapsel gate, an unusual design characteristic of Sussex in which the frame revolves around a central upright (another example can be seen at Pyecombe). Nearby Church Farm is an open farm set in a wonderful downland setting which welcomes pre-booked groups of visitors for organised trailer rides over farmland and through conservation areas. There is also a course fishing lake, open in summer and on some winter evenings.

### *Shoreham-by-Sea*               *Map 2 ref I8*
*5 miles NE of Worthing off the A27*

The ancient port of Shoreham-by-Sea stands at the mouth of the River Adur. There is evidence of both Roman and Saxon occupation here, although it was not until the Norman period that the town became an important river and seaport. At that time, the Adur was navigable as far as Bramber (and for small craft, on up to Shipley) and the main port stood a mile or so upstream from its present position at Old Shoreham. Here, the Normans built a church, *St Nicholas'*, on the foundations of a Saxon predecessor which was later to be restored by the Victorians. The church is surrounded by some handsome old houses.

After 1100, however, the river estuary began to silt up and the old port and toll bridge were abandoned in favour of a new purpose-built site at New Shoreham. The great church of *St Mary de Haura* (meaning 'of the harbour') was built here with huge stone walls and an 80 foot tower. It was one of the largest non-monastic churches of its day, although sadly the nave collapsed in 1720 and was never replaced. The new port then flourished until the 16th century when the growth of a shingle spit diverted the course of the river with economically disastrous results. Shoreham then declined for two centuries until the rise of nearby Brighton and the excavation of a new river course in 1818 led to a revival in the town's fortunes.

To reflect this new found importance, *Shoreham Fort* was constructed at the eastern end of Shoreham Beach as part of Palmerston's coastal defence system. Built around 1854, this half moon shaped lunette was capable of accommodating six muzzle-loading guns which each could fire 80 pounds of shot; in recent years the structure has been restored and is open to visitors free of charge. Today, Shoreham handles three million tons of cargo a year and is well established as the nearest south coast port to London.

Further information on the history of Shoreham can be found at the *Marlipins Museum* on the High Street, a fascinating establishment which is housed in one of the oldest surviving non-religious buildings in the country. During the 14th century this former Norman customs warehouse was given an unusual knapped flint and Caen stone chequerwork facade and has a single 42 foot beam supporting the first floor. The building has been owned by the Sussex Archeological Society since 1929. Along with special maritime and topographical displays, there are good general exhibits on local geology, history and archeology. Shoreham's airport, which is England's oldest, has a lovely art deco terminal and a **Museum of D-Day Aviation**, with engines, artefacts, uniforms and a replica Spitfire.

## Southwick
*Map 2 ref I7*

*2 miles E of Shoreham-by-Sea off the A259*

A beached row boat marks the entrance to **The Pilot Inn**, a welcoming and friendly public house in the seaside town of Southwick. As the story goes, the cruel sea deposited this wave-tossed ship outside the inn; in the swell of the storm the pilot has sworn to himself that he would never again venture from dry land, and spent the rest of his days sitting in his boat outside his favourite inn telling tales of the sea. Even now, so they say, you might see his ghostly

**The Pilot Inn**

form at the prow of his boat. The interior of this cosy establishment continues the nautical theme: naval memorabilia lines the walls, and along one wall the round windows are reminiscent of portholes. And this super pub has much more to offer than a ghost, such as good food, good ales (including Courage and Specked Hen beers) and a warm welcome. The two-tiered restaurant specialises in Thai food, although there are also English staples on the menu, much of it featuring freshly caught fish and local produce. *The Pilot Inn, Station Road, Southwick, West Sussex BN42 4AE Tel: 01273 591789.*

# CHAPTER TWO
## The West Sussex Downs

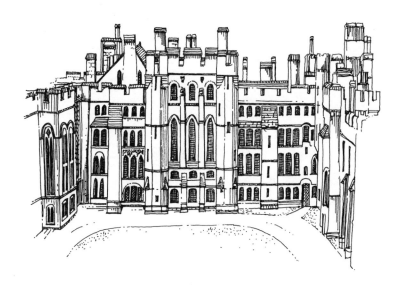

*Arundel Castle*

# Chapter 2 - Area Covered

*For precise location of places please refer to the colour
maps found at the rear of the book.*

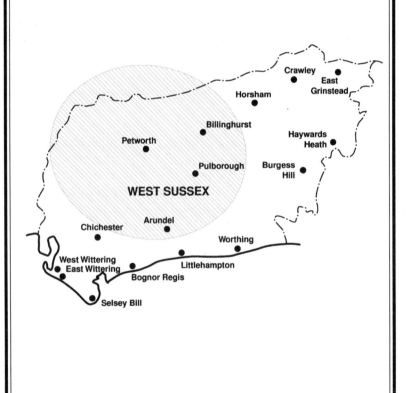

# 2
# *The West Sussex Downs*

## Introduction

The South Downs Way, a nearly 100 mile long bridleway from Winchester and Buriton in the West to Beachy Head in the East, is characterised by expansive views right across the country. This fine chalk downland is peppered with beautiful rural hamlets and villages, with rolling hills, valleys, and spectacular natural beauty.

In the westernmost area of this magnificent part of West Sussex, the country town of Midhurst is home to many fine Elizabethan houses, and borders the impressive 17,000 acre Cowdray Park. In nearby Petworth, a former cloth weaving centre, can be found a a range of fine merchants' and landowners' residences. The National Trust owned Petworth Estate is a majestic example of 'Capability' Brown's landscaping artistry.

The villages of Kirdford and Loxwood border the fertile Weald region. Billingshurst, a sizable country town, was in the days prior to the coming of the railways an important coaching town, and retains several good former coaching inns. The ancient settlement of Pulborough, a mile or so from the confluence of the Rivers Arun and Rother, is a scattered community founded by the Romans as a staging post, and is today a sizable village which is perhaps best known for its excellent freshwater fishing. It is also home to the magnficent Parham Park, perhaps the finest Elizabethan country house in Sussex, in the heart of a great deer park on an open plateau at the foot of the South Downs ridge.

The charming village of West Chiltington and ancient settlement of Amberley are spread out below the steep scarp slope of the South Downs ridge. Here can also be found the handsome village of Storrington, providing good access to the South Downs Way, and Findon, located within the South Downs Area of Outstanding Natural Beauty yet only four miles from the sea.

Another highlight of this delightful region is, of course, the historic and appealing town of Arundel. All this, as well as some fine examples of Roman palaces and villas, as at Bignor, and a perennially mild climate makes the Downlands a popular and justly celebrated choice for all year round touring.

# Midhurst

Midhurst is a lovely, quiet and prosperous market town which stands on a sandstone rise just to the north of the South Downs, near the junction of the A272 and A286.

Its origins lie in the early Middle Ages, and the town has a rich variety of buildings and streets of many types and ages. At St Ann's Hill there can be seen the remains of the once distinguished castle buildings and surrounding earthwork defences, commanding a view of the River Rother.

Among the town's many noteworthy buildings are the tall timber-framed **Elizabeth House**, the 15th century **Spread Eagle** coaching inn, and the 19th century **cottage library** in Knockhundred Row. This delightfully named thoroughfare is believed to have been the focal point for the ancient custom of knocking for 100 militia men when there was a call to defend the town. Midhurst's renowned **Grammar School** was founded in 1672 in the 16th century timber former Market Hall. Over two centuries later, it was attended by the young H G Wells when his mother was a housekeeper at nearby Uppark House. The town is the setting for several of Wells' short stories; in his autobiography Wells wrote, *"Midhurst has always been a happy place for me. I suppose it rained there at times, but all my memories of Midhurst are in sunshine."*

In the town there are a number of good choices of pubs including the Crown in Edinburgh Square, parts of which date back to 1580, the Wheatsheaf at the end of North Street and the Swan.

The exquisite **Redford Cottage** is a bed and breakfast establishment of great distinction. Delightfully situated in the heart of rural Sussex, this haven of peace and tranquillity, although tucked

*Redford Cottage*

away in a quiet corner of the countryside, is only a short distance from all the amenities of the delightful towns of Midhurst, Petworth and Chichester. The self-contained part of the house, called The Engine House, evokes an age before that of town electricity. Taste-fully furnished with an eye always towards cosiness and comfort, this welcoming establishment makes for a wonderful bolt hole for cold winter weekends - with its open fires and comfy chairs - or for long lazy summer days in the shade of the towering trees on the extensive grounds. The picturesque gardens are home to all sorts of animals and beautiful well-manicured lawns, the epitome of the tra-ditional English countryside. Owner Caroline Angela is the warm and friendly proprietor of this superior B & B. *Redford Cottage, Redford, Midhurst, West Sussex GU24 0QF Tel: 01428 741242*

On the other side of the Rother in Midhurst stand the ruins of **Cowdray House**, the once magnificent courtyard mansion built of local sandstone in the early 16th century by the Earl of Southamp-ton on the site of an earlier 13th century manor house. Henry VIII stayed at Cowdray in 1538, and later in the century, Elizabeth I was a regular visitor. On one occasion the Queen and her entourage were said to have consumed three oxen and 140 geese during a week-long stay, no doubt making her departure something of a relief for her overstretched host, Viscount Montague.

In 1793, Cowdray House was gutted by fire and a week later, its owner, the last Lord Montague, was drowned while on a visit to Germany. This fulfilled a legendary curse placed on the owners of Cowdray House by a monk evicted from Battle Abbey by the first

**Cowdray Park**

owner during Henry VIII's Dissolution of the Monasteries. Today, visitors can view the roofless remains of the east side of the quadrangle court, along with parts of the west side where the turreted three-storey gatehouse remains largely intact. The 17,000 acre **Cowdray Park** is one of the largest private estates in Sussex and is a well established for venue for polo ever weekend and some weekdays from the end of April until mid-July.

### Easebourne

*Map 1 ref D4*

*1 mile NE of Midhurst off the A272*

The delightful estate village of Easebourne lies a mile along the A272 to the northeast of Midhurst. This is the site of fragments of a former Augustinian **nunnery** of the Blessed Virgin Mary and its adjoining church of St Mary. The nunnery was founded in the 13th century and prospered until 1478, when the prioress and two of her nuns were accused of 'gross immorality' and of squandering the income of the priory on 'hunting and extravagant entertaining'. Parts of the mediaeval institution have survived as the parish church, vicarage and garden. Along with its picturesque collection of yellow painted estate cottages, Easebourne contains another building with a unusual history, **Budgenor Lodge**. This was built in 1793 as a model workhouse for the Easebourne union of parishes and in its day, was much admired by groups of visiting dignitaries.

## Lurgashall
*Map 1 ref D4*

*3 miles NE of Midhurst off the A286*

This attractive small village boasts an unusual loggia outside the predominantly Saxon (11th century) church, where parishioners who had travelled from afar could eat the provisions they had brought with them on their journeys. The large stone in the porch was once used to protect new graves from body-snatchers. The 17th century font is made of Sussex marble.

## Lodsworth
*Map 1 ref D4*

*3 miles NE of Midhurst off the A272*

This pleasant community lies beside the River Lod, a small tributary of the River Rother. The village contains some attractive buildings, including a manor house dating from the 13th century, an early 18th century Dower House, and a more recent country residence known as the Great House. The village church of St Peter occupies a wonderful site with views across the valley. Down the hill, just to the north of the church, St Peter's Well is said according to legend to contain healing waters.

## Fernhurst
*Map 1 ref D3*

*4 miles N of Midhurst off the A286*

Fernhurst is blessed with a lovely village green surrounded by an assortment of tile-hung cottages.

Just to the east, **Black Down** (or Blackdown Hill) rises abruptly from the Sussex Weald. The slopes of this 919 foot National Trust owned sandstone hill are covered in heather, gorse, silver birch and Scots pine, creating an ideal environment for a variety of upland birdlife. The summit of Black Down is the highest point in Sussex; from here there are spectacular views over the Weald and South Downs all the way to the English Channel. A particularly good viewpoint is the group of firs on the southern crest known as the **Temple of the Winds**. One of the paths leading to the top of Black Down is known as **Tennyson's Lane**, after the famous poet who lived for 20 years at Aldworth House on hill's the eastern slope.

At one time a Royal Navy signal tower stood on **Tally Knob**, a prominent outcrop which lies to the southeast of the Temple of the Winds. As a development of their tried and tested system of fire beacons, in 1796 the Admiralty introduced the Shutter Telegraph as a more sophisticated means of passing messages between Portsmouth and London. Though ingenious, the system was found to be impractical and was soon abandoned.

**The King's Arms** in Fernhurst is a handsome, traditional 17th century free house and restaurant serving genuine Dublin Guinness, a superb range of real ales and freshly prepared meals using local ingredients. Set on a main road amidst rolling farmland, not far from Goodwood Racecourse, this welcoming establishment is run by sisters Lucy and Annabel, Lucy's husband Brian and Annabel's

*The King's Arms*

husband Michael. Lucy and Michael do the cooking; having been chefs in London for nearly 10 years they bring their expertise to the bar meals and the restaurant's excellent and innovative menu, which includes dishes such as steak with handcut chips, pan-fried halibut and lobster ravioli. Everything is fresh and home-made, from the salad dressings to the ice creams. There are five real ales (including two 'guest beers' at any one time), changing seasonally, and an extensive wine list. The atmosphere is friendly and congenial, the service efficient. The cosy interior boasts low oak-beamed ceilings and a large inglenook fireplace in the restaurant area. Open seven days a week. *The King's Arms, Midhurst Road, Fernhurst, West Sussex GU27 3HA Tel: 01428 652005.*

## Marley Common

Map 1 ref C3

*5 miles N of Midhurst off the A286*

Just over the Surrey/Sussex border, Marley Common is a broad stretch of National Trust owned sandstone heathland which affords some fine views over the Weald to the South Downs. **Shottermill Ponds**, a pair of interesting hammer ponds, can be found at the foot of nearby Marley Lane.

## *Trotton*                                    *Map 1 ref C5*
*3 miles W of Midhurst off the A272*

The broad valley of the River Rother to the west of Midhurst was once a densely wooded area known for its timber and charcoal production. At Trotton there is an impressive five-arched bridge, the money for which was provided by Thomas, the first Lord Camoys, who accompanied Henry V on the Agincourt campaign. Completed in the early 1400s, it still carries the busy main road.

Most of the older buildings in Trotton, including the bridge, are constructed of local honey coloured sandstone. The bridge dates from about 1400 and still carries traffic over the river Rother. The ancient **Church of St George** stands beside Trotton Bridge; dating mainly from the 12th century, its west wall contains an exceptional series of murals depicting Christ in Judgement and the Seven Deadly Sins. There are also two very fine monumental brasses: one to Margaret, Lady Camoys (dating from around 1310, this is believed to be the earliest such memorial to be dedicated to a woman), and one to the first Lord Camoys and his second wife, Elizabeth, who was the widow of Sir Harry 'Hotspur' Percy. The door jambs of the west door are pitted with curious indentations which are thought to have been made by local bowmen honing their arrows before Sunday archery practice.

## *Durford Abbey*                              *Map 1 ref B4*
*5 miles W of Midhurst off the A272*

The site of the now demolished **Durford Abbey** also lies close to the county border. This isolated monastery was founded in the 12th century by a community of Premonstratensian monks, a strict vegetarian order which was founded in 1120 by St Norbert at Premontre in France. Unlike other institutions, which grew hugely wealthy on income from their monastic estates, life at Durford seemed more a matter of survival. In fact, so harsh was the monk's existence that on dissolving the monastery in 1539, Thomas Cromwell's commissioner described Durford as *"the poorest abbey I have seen, far in debt and in decay"*.

Although little of the original abbey now remains, the canons of Durford succeeded in leaving an important legacy in the form of three 15th century bridges over the River Rother. (During the mediaeval period, it was a duty of religious houses to provide and maintain such bridges.) Both **Maidenmarsh Bridge** near the site of the abbey and **Habin Bridge** to the south of Rogate are worth a visit; the latter still carries the road to South Harting and consists of four semi-circular arches interspersed with massive stone cutwaters.

## *South Harting*                    Map 1 ref B5
*7 miles W of Midhurst off the B2141*

South Harting, with its ancient thatched cottages, flint walls and unusually wide main street of fine Georgian houses and 17th century cottages, must be one of the most attractive village in the South Downs. A twisting three mile journey from Habin Bridge, South Harting is the largest of the three settlements known collectively as the Hartings. Writer Anthony Trollope spent the last two years of his life here, during which time he created four novels. A pen and paper-knife belonging to the acclaimed 19th century novelist can be seen in the village ***Church of St Mary and St Gabriel***.

South Harting's famous church spire is faced with copper shingles, creating a bright verdigris hue which can be seen for miles. Memorials in the church include several to the former owners of the nearby downland estate, Uppark, including one to Sir Henry Fetherstonhaugh. The distinctive war memorial in the churchyard was carved in Portland stone by the renowned modern sculptor and typographer, Eric Gill. Near the entrance to the churchyard, an ancient set of parish stocks can also be found, along with a whipping post complete with three pairs of wrist irons.

South Harting stands at the foot of ***Harting Down*** beneath the steep scarp slope of the South Downs ridge. The ridge is traversed by the ***South Downs Way***, the spectacular long-distance footpath which stretches for nearly 100 miles from Winchester and Buriton in the west to Beachy Head in the east. Here, the path skirts around ***Beacon Hill***, which at 793 feet above sea level is one of the highest points in the Downs. A 2,500 year old rectangular Iron Age hill fort surrounds the summit; there are spectacular views from the surviving ramparts over the Weald to the north and as far as Chichester's harbour and Cathedral to the south.

This very pretty village is also a good setting off point for scenic drives along the B2141 and B2146, and the South Downs footway through East Harting, Elsted and Cocking.

Said to be one of the oldest cottages in South Harting and once part of the Uppark estate, the charming ***South Gardens Cottage*** is a beautiful 16th century timbered, thatched cottage offering bed and breakfast. The traditional interior features exposed beams and large open fireplaces. The cottage, originally two, is newly restored and beautifully furnished; the fabrics and furniture have been chosen with great care. The guests' dining room is particularly attractive. There is plenty of parking and a large garden, with a gate leading to three lakes and a path to the village. In the other direc-

**South Gardens Cottage**

tion, a short walk through woods leads to the South Downs Way or the National Trust house, Uppark. The owners Mr and Mrs Holmes and their animals will soon make you feel at home in this lovely setting. Mrs Holmes is an art dealer specialising in antique maps and old and new prints of the countryside and animals; these may be viewed on request. *South Gardens Cottage, South Harting, West Sussex GU31 5QJ Tel: 01730 825040.*

### Graffham                                        *Map 1 ref D5*
*2 miles SE of Midhurst off the A272*
This scenic rural community spread out along the foot of the Downs escarpment is home to the famous Lavington Stud.

### Heyshott                                        *Map 1 ref D5*
*2 miles SE of Midhurst off the A272*
Just half a mile from Graffham and only 5 minutes' drive from the historic town of Midhurst and within easy distance of Goodwood, Singleton, Chichester and the West Sussex coast, the beautiful period house, **Amberfold**, offers accommodation in the tiny and scenic hamlet of Heyshott. The house dates back to Tudor times and is surrounded by miles of open countryside, ideal for nature lovers, walkers and bird-watchers. Proprietors Annabelle and Alexander Costaras have put careful thought and every consideration into making a stay here, for a weekend or longer, the perfect retreat. The accommodation in this charming 17th century listed building comprises a totally self-contained annexe, where guests can come

*Amberfold*

and go as they please. The oak-beamed ceilings add immeasurably to the warm and welcoming ambience; the double bedroom with en-suite facilities features every modern convenience guests have come to expect. A lavishly stocked refrigerator, replenished daily, is provided for self-catering continental breakfast. *Amberfold, Heyshott, Near Midhurst, West Sussex GU29 0DA  Tel: 01730 812385*

### Tillington
*Map 1 ref E5*

*4 miles E of Midhurst off the A272*

The charming village of Tillington is bordered by the famous wall around Petworth Park and dates back to the Domesday Book, when it was called Tolinstone. At the highest point of the village stands the fine 12th century parish church of **All Hallows** with its imposing Scots Crown tower. This church has been depicted in paintings by Turner and Constable.

## Petworth

Five miles east of Midhurst off the A272, the historic town of Petworth stands on the crest of a sandstone ridge. Between the 14th and 16th centuries, Petworth was an important cloth-weaving centre; a number of fine merchants' and landowners' residences, including Daintrey House, North House and Tudor House, can be seen in its narrow streets. The cramped Market Place contains a fine late 18th century arcaded town hall and a striking bank building, the National Westminster, built in baroque style in 1901. Other noteworthy buildings include the Somerset Almshouses (or Upper Hospital), built in 1746 for 12 widows, each of whom received a princely pension of 10 pounds per year.

Situated in the rolling South Downs the 350 acre **Burton Park Farm** is easily accessible but far from the madding crowd. The comfortable farmhouse provides a combination of seclusion and relaxation. It nestles amongst the Poplars and has wonderful views of the Downs throughout the seasons. There are approximately 90 species of birds in this area and some of these may be seen when breakfasting in the large conservatory used by the guests. Mrs DeHeger is a

**Burton Park Farm**

warm but not intrusive host who hopes to cater for most requirements. All rooms have ensuite bathrooms and are furnished with tea and coffee facilities; vegetarians are catered for. Guests here have the opportunity of visiting a wide range of interesting places nearby, including the Roman Villa, Petworth, Arundel and Chichester, all different but delightful. After a day exploring you can enjoy an evening meal at one of the many local pubs/restaurants, some of which are within walking distance. *Burton Park Farm, Petworth, West Sussex GU28 0JT Tel: 01798 342431*

The most dominant feature of Petworth is the grand house and park which together make up the National Trust owned Petworth Estate. Surrounded by a wall over 13 miles long, the 700 acre **Petworth Park** was landscaped by Lancelot 'Capability' Brown in the 1750s. The sweeping grounds contain many stately trees, a lake and deer park, and command views still recognisable as those celebrated by Turner.

**Petworth House** was built between 1688 and 1696 on the site of a 13th century manor house, the present building incorporating the original medieval chapel and hall undercroft. The house, with its magnificent 320 foot west front, was built in French style on the instructions of Charles, Sixth Duke of Somerset. The design has been attributed to the Architect Daniel Marot, except for the south front which was added in 1869-72 to a design by Anthony Salvin. The magnificent galleries and state rooms of this splendid old house are filled with one of the finest art collections in the country, including works by Dutch old masters such as Rembrandt and Van Dyck, and 20 paintings by Turner, a frequent visitor in his day. Other work on show includes paintings by Holbein, Blake, Reynolds and Gainsborough. Additional treasures are the grand staircase with its elegant frescoes and some outstanding examples of the work of the master carver, Grinling Gibbons.

Returning to the A285 and crossing the River Rother at Coultershaw Bridge, one of the earliest pumped water systems was installed here in 1790 to pipe water the two mile distance to Petworth. The **Coultershaw Water Wheel and Beam Pump** is now a scheduled ancient monument which has been restored to working condition by the Sussex Industrial Archeology Society. The beam pump can still be seen in operation, and there is also an exhibition giving some interesting background information on water supply, pumps and local natural history.

**The British School of Ballooning** just north of Petworth organises champagne balloon trips over the countryside; Tel. 01428 707307.

## Selham                                             *Map 1 ref E4*
*1 mile N of Petworth off the A283*

The tiny hamlet of Selham, near Petworth, is the peaceful and secluded location for **Manor Farm**. A working dairy farm, it also offers high quality bed and breakfast and can be considered a reprieve from the more well-trodden tourist route of the South Downs. This beautiful 600 year old building is impressive both outside and in.

**Manor Farm**

With its cosy and inviting traditional farmhouse interior, complete with flagstone floors, and a wonderful old fireplace found during renovations, it makes an ideal getaway. The bedrooms boast original wooden beams, whilst the kitchen has a huge old wooden table and of course an Aga stove. Down on the farm there is a fresh-water pond and views of great natural beauty across Cowdray Park, home of polo. Owner Davina Comber takes pleasure in ensuring guests feel at home; her home-cooked breakfasts are delicious. Guests enjoy their own entrance and sitting room to ensure they can make the most of their privacy and relaxation during their stay. Children are particularly welcome. *Manor Farm, Selham, Petworth, West Sussex GU28 0PP Tel: 01798 861320.*

## Fittleworth
*Map 1 ref E5*

*2 miles SE of Petworth off the A283*

A little further to the southeast, Fittleworth is a village of charming sandstone buildings stretching down to the River Rother. The noted composer Sir Edward Elgar lived near Fittleworth for some years, writing his Cello Concerto during this time.

**Street Farm** is a superior bed and breakfast hotel with great character located in Fittleworth, in the heart of the Sussex countryside on the B2138 between Petworth and Arundel. Converted just over 10 years ago from the barn and outbuildings of an 18th century dairy farm, using locally quarried stone - the dining room occupies what was once the milk store - this relaxing B&B offers very roomy accommodation in handsomely furnished rooms with good views over the South Downs. With the coast and countryside on the doorstep, your hosts Martin and Joanne Sturgis are happy to provide maps,

**Street Farm**

information and itineraries for walks and bird-watching in the area, and even a picnic lunch on request - Galahad, the family's retriever, will happily accompany you on your trek. The owners will also be pleased to recommend their favourites from among the excellent restaurants and public houses in the village and surrounding area. *Street Farm, Lower Street, Fittleworth, West Sussex RH20 1EN Tel: 01798 865721*

Here in this secluded and picturesque village setting, **The Swan Inn** is a charming and traditional rural hotel surrounded by forests and hills, with the South Downs Way for a backdrop. Handy for the business and leisure traveller - Gatwick and Southampton airports are less than an hour away, the railway station at Pulborough only two miles away, Arundel eight miles distant, and the centres of Horsham and Chichester 15 miles off - the Swan combines the best

**The Swan Inn**

in traditional coaching inn standards with modern facilities usually associated with much larger establishments. The stately building dates back to 1382; the interior, with its open log fires and exposed oak-beamed ceilings, is welcoming and peaceful. Here, an informal and relaxed atmosphere goes hand in hand with first-class service. There are 11 tastefully furnished guest bedrooms, two with four-poster beds. In the Picture Room, 33 original works of art, each one painted in situ and extremely valuable, grace the walls. In the cosy oak-beamed restaurant, hearty breakfasts, lunches, delicious after-noon tea, tempting evening meals and light suppers are served with style. *The Swan Inn, Lower Street, Fittleworth, West Sussex RH20 1EN Tel: 01798 865429 Fax: 01798 865546.*

## Stopham                                            *Map 2 ref F5*
*3 miles SE of Petworth off the A283*

Stopham is the family home of the Barttelot family, an old Norman family who still reside in Stopham House. The Barttelots are strongly associated with the building of the early 15th century **Stopham Bridge**, an impressive stone structure which is widely regarded as the finest medieval bridge in Sussex. The tall central arch was re-built in 1822 to allow masted vessels to pass upstream towards the Wey and Arun Canal.

## Bignor                                             *Map 1 ref E6*
*5 miles S of Petworth off the A285*

Bignor's central thoroughfares are arranged in an uneven square. The village contains some wonderful domestic buildings, including the photogenic 15th century Old Shop - a two-storey thatched house whose ramshackle timber-framed walls are infilled with brick, flint and plaster.

Bignor is best known for having been the administrative centre of a large Roman agricultural estate, the focus of which was a siz-able villa which was accidentally uncovered by a farmer's plough in 1811. Excavations revealed the foundations of *Bignor Roman Villa*, one of the largest villas discovered so far. A grand courtyard resi-dence covering four and a half acres which was inhabited between the 1st and 4th centuries, the most striking feature of the building is its floor mosaics. These include depictions of gladiators, Diana, Venus, Ganymede and Medusa, and in the north corridor, there is an 82 foot mosaic pavement which is the longest of its type in the British Isles. Visitors can see excavations going on in summer.

Stane Street, the remarkably straight Roman road which once connected the important administrative centre of Londinium with the port of Chichester, 57 miles away, now confined to just a path, cuts right across the beautiful downland nearby.

## Wisborough Green
*Map 2 ref F4*

*4 miles NE of Petworth off the A272*

This wonderfully open village has a huge rectangular tree-lined village green covering nine acres, making it one of the largest in the country. The village church of St Peter Ad Vincula (St Peter in chains) stands near the circular village pond. This handsome building contains a fine medieval wall painting which was covered over in the 13th century during the rebuilding of the chancel arch and was only rediscovered by accident in 1867.

If you are thinking of finding a place to stay while in Wisborough Green or exploring the surrounding area, *Strood Green Cottage*, built around 1650 on part of the Mitford Estate, has an air of arcadian peace and tranquillity. Retaining original oak beams and large open

*Strood Green Cottage*

fireplaces, a stay in this relaxing and evocative family home, now offering bed and breakfast, is a bit like a journey into the past. From the panelled low beamed entrance hall is a tantalising glimpse of an Italian influenced courtyard where breakfast and tea can be taken in the summer. Beyond the profuse cottage garden, lawns run down to the woodland, where guests are free to wander.

For the more energetic, extensive walks can be taken in the neighbouring ancient woods. Horses can be stabled, and dogs are welcome. Racing enthusiasts are catered for, as proprietor Mrs Janet Martin Sadler is a member of Goodwood Racecourse and the Syndicate Good Racecourse Owners Group. The bedrooms are supremely comfortable and the breakfasts excellent. Mrs Sadler will provide you with detailed directions if you ring in advance - essential if you are not to miss the turning into this delightful cottage. *Strood Green Cottage, Strood Green, Near Wisborough Green, Billingshurst, West Sussex RH14 0HL Tel: 01403 700362*

To the west of Wisborough Green there are two areas of preserved woods, together amounting to 400 acres, which are in the care of the Sussex Wildlife Trust. These ancient Wealden woodlands provide an indication of how most of Sussex north of the Downs would have looked before the arrival of modern humankind.

Present day visitors to this peaceful rural landscape may find it hard to imagine that in the 16th and 17th centuries this area was an important industrial centre. Thanks to the seemingly limitless supply of trees for fuel, iron foundries and forges prospered throughout the area right up until the Industrial Revolution. A plentiful local supply of high quality sand also led to a number of early glassworks being set up at Kirdford, Wisborough Green and Loxwood. During the 16th century, Huguenot settlers from France and the Low Countries introduced new and improved methods of glass manufacture, and the industry flourished until 1616 when lobbying by rival shipbuilding and iron-smelting interests led to government legislation banning glass-makers from using timber to fuel their furnaces.

## *Kirdford*                                           *Map 2 ref F4*
*4 miles NE of Petworth off the A272*

In the beautiful village of Kirdford, the ***Half Moon Inn*** is a welcoming and handsome brick-built country pub and restaurant dating back to the mid 1600s. Set along a quiet country lane, this traditional establishment features a multitude of exposed beams, a large inglenook fireplace and an abundance of attractive polished horse brasses. A Free House, the Half Moon offers a choice of superb real

***Half Moon Inn***

ales - but it is the food people come in droves for (you will have to book well in advance for a table). Fish is a house speciality: owner Jim Moran has family connections with Billingsgate fishmarket in London, and is a connoisseur of fine fish - a fact reflected in the wide choice of fresh fish available at all times. Steaks, game, and poultry dishes also feature on the menu. This excellent establishment also boasts two supremely comfortable guest rooms, should visitors care to extend their stay. There is riding from the village, superb walks, and opportunities for birdwatching, clay pigeon shooting, golf and boules in the immediate area. *Half Moon Inn, Kirdford, Nr Billingshurst, West Sussex RH14 0LT Tel: 01403 820223*

Kirdford has always been the centre of several industrial activities, including glass-making, iron-working and the quarrying of Petworth marble. It has a 12th century church and some fine tile-fronted cottages set along a green and pleasant tree-lined avenue.

Another burgeoning industry is to be found at *Kirdford Growers*, a co-operative of 15 apple growers in Sussex, Dorset and Somerset. The longest established apple and pear co-operative in the country - the first apple juice was bottled in the village as long ago as 1938 - the old farm press has been replaced by modern hygenic equipment, though the character of the juice still reflects the quality of the famous local orchards. The growers' country shop on site sells top Sussex fruit and the home-produced and delicious Kirdford

**Kirdford Growers**

Apple Juice: Bramley is dry with a good balance of fruit acids and a light fruitiness; Cox is sweeter, with a hint of pear; the even sweeter Russet has a fragile floweriness and a lingering tang; they also produce a Sussex juice, a blend of Cox and Bramley apples. There is also a good range of other country produce and gift ideas: fresh fruit and vegetables, home-baked breads, farmhouse cheeses, jams, pickles and ice creams; as well as wines and ciders, greeting cards and many gift ideas. Open Monday-Saturday 9-5; Sunday 10-5. *Kirdford Growers Country Shop, Kirdford, West Sussex RH14 0NQ Tel: 01403 820274.*

**The Foresters Arms** is a very pleasant hostely in Kirdford offering excellent King & Barnes ales, a superb choice of meals and, if desired, a relaxing and comfortable stay in one of the three guest rooms available - including one which comprises a wonderful, roomy family suite with separate sitting room. Built in the 1550s, this secluded and cosy pub with its exposed timbers and low ceilings makes the perfect country retreat - popular with locals and visitors alike. Your hosts Christopher and Mo Timmis have adorned the walls of this charming establishment with handsome oil paintings and watercol-

*The Forresters Arms*

ours depicting lively country scenes. The home-prepared and home-cooked meals are served in the farmhouse-style dining room. There is stabling adjacent for two horses, with good riding from the pub and into the surrounding scenic countryside. Good walking is also available. The pub also has a large, restful garden.*The Foresters Arms, Kirdford, West Sussex RH14 0DN  Tel: 01403 820205*

## Loxwood
*Map 2 ref F3*

*6 miles NE of Petworth off the B2138*

Loxwood is a small and very pretty village on the Sussex/Surrey border. Once home to an extremely rare timber-framed church, some of the original wooden pews were transferred to its late 19th century replacement. The nearby Onslow Arms stands beside the **Wey and Arun Junction Canal,** the inland waterway which was opened in 1816 to link London with the south coast at Littlehampton. In common with most British canals, the coming of the railways sounded its death knell and in 1871, it was closed. Certain stretches are now restored, offering the opportunity to cruise genly along one of Britain's most scenic canals. The Canal Restoration Trust, the organisation behind the restoration, also publishes a useful guide to the canal-side footpath.

Loxwood is the former base of the *'Society of Dependents'*, a puritanical sect founded in 1850 by the former London evangelist, John Sirgood. The group became known as the *'Cokelers'* because of their preference for cocoa over alcohol.

**Strudgwick Farmhouse** is an extensive and distinguished bed and breakfast guest house located in theattractive rural community of Loxwood. Set in five acres of secluded and tranquil grounds, the accommodation in this desirable house comprises a self contained

**Strudgwick Farmhouse**

suite on the top floor, most suitable for self-catering, with comfortable lounge (and bed settee), open-plan fully equipped kitchen, twin bedroom, a shower room and wc, as well as a south facing balcony; a first-floor large single room and on the ground floor a double/family room ensuite, and a twin bedroom with private bathroom.

The guests' lounge/breakfast room has french doors opening onto a sunny south-facing terrace. All rooms have colour TV and tea making facilities. Margaret and Hugh Douglas the charming owners take great care over providing guests with every comfort. Their hospitality is in evidence throughout this attractive home. The furnishings are superb, every room is decorated with flair. In the garden guests can relax and enjoy the visiting wild life to the sound of the fountain and water cascading through the rockery into the ornamental pond stocked with water lilies. There are several good pubs and a vegetarian restaurant nearby, and lots of wooded and canal walks with a golf course within minutes in the secluded and superior location. *Strudgwick Farm, Loxwood, Billingshurst, West Sussex RH14 0TZ  Tel: 01403 752444*

## Rudgwick
*Map 2 ref G3*

*10 miles NE of Petworth off the A281*

The characteristic Wealden settlement of Rudgwick is a charming village of attractive tile-fronted cottages standing on high ground surrounded by woodland. The 14th century village church has some delicate carved tracery and there are some fine views southwards to Chanctonbury Ring.

# Billingshurst

This attractive small town stands at the junction of the A272 and the A29 London to Bognor Regis road, eight miles northeast of Petworth. In the days prior to the coming of the railways, Billingshurst was an important coaching town and several good former coaching inns, including the half-timbered 16th century *Olde Six Bells*, can still be found in the old streets. The Norman *Church of St Mary's* suffered the same fate as many of its contemporaries and was heavily 'restored' during the Victorian era; however, it still retains its original 120 foot eight sided spire which, since 1884, has featured a clock whose mechanism is a half-sized replica of Big Ben's. The *Unitarian chapel* built in 1754 is one of the oldest of its kind in southern England. A recently opened *Sotheby's* auction house is located at Summers Place on the main road to Horsham.

## Shipley
*Map 2 ref G5*

*5 miles SE of Billingshurst off the A272*

The parish church at Shipley contains some fine 12th century features and a wonderful alabaster memorial to Sir Thomas Caryll and his family. The village also features a small disused toll house and a distinctive hammer pond which in the 16th century would have supplied water to drive the bellows and mechanical hammers in an adjacent iron foundry.

Shipley is perhaps best known, however, for being the former home of the celebrated Sussex writer Hilaire Belloc, who lived in the house next to the local landmark *King's Mill* from 1906 until his death in 1953. This great five storey white smock mill which is open to the public on a limited number of days each year; now restored, a memorial plaque to its former owner hangs above the entrance. Nearby stand the ruins of *Knepp Castle*, a mansion built by John Nash in 1809.

## Pulborough
*Map 2 ref F5*

*5 miles SW of Billingshurst off the A29*

The ancient settlement of Pulborough stands a mile or so from the confluence of the Rivers Arun and Rother. This scattered community was founded by the Romans as a staging post, or *mansio,* on Stane Street, the arterial road which once connected London with Chichester. Despite its strategically important location beside the Arun river crossing, Pulborough failed to grow like some of its rivals, and today it remains a sizable village which is perhaps best known for its excellent freshwater fishing. It also retains some fine early buildings; **Walberton House** (1803) was designed by Robert Smirke, the architect of the British Museum in London.

The magnficent **Parham Park**, probably the finest Elizabethan country house in Sussex, stands in the heart of a great deer park on an open plateau at the foot of the South Downs ridge. Designed in the classic 'E' shape, the mansion was built in the 1570s for Sir Thomas Palmer, a wealthy cloth merchant, on the site of a smaller monastic house which once belonged to Westminster Abbey.

Parham contains one of the finest Elizabethan interiors in the country. The magnificent state rooms, including the 160 foot Long Gallery, Great Hall and Great Parlour, feature mullioned windows and wood panelled walls, and are furnished with an exceptional collection of period furniture, oriental carpets, rare needlework and fine paintings. The house is surrounded by seven acres of wooded parkland containing a statue garden, lake, picnic enclosure and a beautiful four acre walled garden with traditional herb beds.

The diminutive church of St Peter stands close to the main house; rebuilt early in the 19th century, its interior features carved ceilings, an unusual lead font and a set of high box pews. The squire's pew had its own fireplace which he was reputed to stoke loudly when the vicar's sermon was becoming tiresome.

## Hardham
*Map 2 ref F5*

*6 miles SW of Billingshurst off the A29*

The village of Hardham is well worth a visit for its Saxon church of **St Botolph** (one of the few churches in the area, it seems, not dedicated to St Mary). This exceptional little building contains a near complete series of wall paintings dating from the early 12th century which are believed to be the earliest examples of their kind in Britain. The murals are thought to have been painted by a team of artists based at St Pancras Priory in Lewes, who were also responsible for those at Coombes and Clayton, further to the southeast. The site of ***Hardham Priory***, a small Augustinian monastic house, lies close by and from here it is possible to join a footpath leading to the disused ***Hardham Tunnel***, a channel which was built to provide a short-cut for river barges wishing to avoid the broad eastern loop of the Arun.

## West Chiltington                                    *Map 2 ref G5*
*4 miles S of Billingshurst off the B2139*

The Norman Church of St Mary in the charming village of West Chiltington has an oak-shingled spire and a roof of Horsham stone. Inside there are some fine wall paintings created between the 12th and 14th centuries but only rediscovered in 1882. The church also possesses an unusually long squint, or *hagioscope*, a narrow angled opening in the wall which allows a view of the main altar from the south aisle. A former glass-making and iron-smelting centre, the village has an interesting industrial and social history, further details of which can be obtained at the ***West Chiltington Museum*** in Church Street. The village stocks and whipping post are preserved outside the church.

***The Elephant & Castle*** public house occupies a quiet location in West Chiltington. Redeveloped but unspoilt, this marvellous country pub retains a charming cottage atmosphere. The handsome flint building dates back to 1665. Originally a cottage dwelling belonging to the church of St Mary's, it has been a pub since 1830 when one Jacob Girling, the son of a wheelwright and saddler who had purchased the house from the church for use as a private dwelling,

***The Elephant & Castle***

obtained a beer licence (accomplished in those days simply by pay-
ing 2 guineas to the Department of Excise). The pub's name derives
from its popularity with local Cutlers - the castle being their trade-
mark and the elephant the symbol of their connections with the
ivory trade. Proprietor Charles Hollingworth is a gregarious and
lively host. Charles is also the cook, and as he is South African by
birth, South African dishes - such as the intriguingly named *boerie*
and *bobotie* - are always on offer, along with traditional English
fare, all home-prepared and home-cooked - to be accompanied, of
course, by the real ales on tap. *The Elephant & Castle, Church Street,
West Chiltington, West Sussex Tel: 01798 813307.*

## *Amberley*                                               Map 2 ref F6
*10 miles SW of Billingshurst off the B2139*

The ancient settlement of Amberley consists of a delightful assortment of flint, brick, stone, timber and thatched cottages spread out
below the steep scarp slope of the South Downs ridge. The village
church of St Michael is thought to have been founded by St Wilfrid,
the missionary who converted the South Saxons to Christianity.
Rebuilt in the 12th century by Bishop Luffa of Chichester at around
the same time as Chichester Cathedral, the church interior contains some strong Norman features. The murals to the right of the
chancel arch date from the time of a further remodelling in the 13th
century. The five bells in the tower, hung in 1742, are said to have
the sweetest peal in the land.

Nearby **Amberley Castle** began life in the 12th century as a
fortified summer palace for the bishops of Chichester. More a manor
house than a castle, alterations over the centuries have included
the construction of a great curtain wall to enclose the entire mano-
rial site. Charles II is believed to have stayed here en route to a safe
haven in France following his defeat at the Battle of Worcester in
1651. The building now operates as a privately run hotel and restaurant.

The series of water meadows to the north of the village are known
as the **Amberley Wild Brooks**. Often flooded and inaccessible by
car, this 30 acre conservation area and nature reserve is a haven for
bird, animal and plantlife. Trains on the Arun Valley line cross the
marshes along specially constructed embankments which were considered engineering marvels of their day when the line was opened
in 1863. Amberley railway station lies a mile to the southwest of the
village at Houghton Bridge, the point where the South Downs way
crosses the River Arun.

Houghton Bridge is also the location of the renowned *Amberley Chalk Pits Museum*, a working museum of industrial history featuring a narrow gauge industrial railway, a collection of vintage motor buses, and a range of workshops which offer live demonstrations of traditional rural trades, including blacksmithing, pottery-making, printing, boat-building and ironmongery. This fascinating 36 acre open air museum is a must for all those with an interest in industrial archeology or transport history.

During the 18th and 19th centuries, chalk was quarried at Amberley for shipping to the many lime kilns which could then be found throughout the lime-deficient farming areas of southern England. Later, large quantities of chalk were needed to supply a new industrial process which involved the high-temperature firing of chalk with small amounts of clay. The revolutionary product resulting from this process was named *'Portland Cement'*, and the Amberley Chalk Pits Museum includes an exhibition on the background and history of this invaluable building material.

### Storrington                                    *Map 2 ref G6*
*8 miles S of Billingshurst off the B2139*

This handsome village provides good access to the South Downs Way near Kithurst Hill. The nearby dry chalk valley known as *Chantry Bottom* is a deserted settlement which was populated by Iron Age, Roman and mediaeval people. The *Church of St Mary the Virgin* dates from the 11th century, though it has had to undergo extensive restoration over the years, as when the steeple collapsed in 1931 after being struck by lightning. The village pond is a peaceful and scenic place to stop for a rest.

### Sullington                                     *Map 3 ref G6*
*9 miles S of Billingshurst off the A283*

The hamlet of Sullington contains a barn which at 115 feet long rivals many of the tithe barns which were a feature of mediaeval monastic estates. This exceptional building has a braced tie-beam roof and, though privately-owned, can be viewed by appointment. On the other side of the main road a mile to the north, *Sullington Warren* is a sandy area of National Trust owned heathland once was used for the farming of rabbits.

### Ashington                                      *Map 2 ref G6*
*7 miles SE of Billingshurst off the A24*

Ashington has some very interesting old buildings, including the Church of St Peter and St Paul, and *Broadbridge Farmstead*, a lovely cottage building that is part brick, part tile-hung and part timbered. The barn next door was once a mill. Ashington contains an unexpected attraction, half a mile north of the village itself. The **Holly Gate Cactus Garden** is an unusual collection of over 20,000 cacti and succulents from the hot and arid regions of the world and has been built up over 30 years by a private enthusiast whose hobby has turned into a living museum. The cacti, many of which can be seen in flower, are laid out in a 'natural' landscaped setting in a series of glasshouses covering a total area of over 10,000 square feet.

## Washington                                    *Map 2 ref G6*
*9 miles SE of Billingshurst off the A24*
The village of Washington stands at the northern end of the Findon Gap, the ancient pass through the Downs. Despite its American-sounding connotations, the name of this peaceful village is derived from the Saxon term for *'settlement of the family of Wassa'*. Thankfully now bypassed by the main road, Washington's varied assortment of buildings reflect its location between the chalk Downs and sandstone Weald. Standing in a picturesque position at one end of the village street, the castellated 15th century Church of St Mary retains its fine Tudor tower despite being heavily 'restored' during the 19th century. This picturesque village is also home to the Frankland Arms, a traditional inn dating back to 1820 and the only pub in the village.

One of the most striking landmarks in Sussex is located within a few yards of the South Downs Way on the southeastern side of Washington. The hill fort at **Chanctonbury Ring** can be seen from miles around in every direction and is a well-known landmark because of the beech trees around its perimeter. These were planted in 1760 by Charles Goring when he was still a boy; in later years, Sir Charles, as he became, inherited Chanctonbury Hill along with Wiston Park, the part 16th, part 19th century mansion lying at the foot of the hill to the northeast which is now run as a conference centre by the Foreign Office. The four acre hilltop site was first occupied by Iron Age people who surrounded it with a ditch and a fortified earthen bank. Centuries later, the Romans built a temple and shrine near its centre, some new remains of which were discovered after several trees had sadly been uprooted during the devastating storm of October 1987

A characteristic downland dew pond lies within a few yards of the South Downs Way just to the west of Chanctonbury Ring. Now restored and maintained by the Society of Sussex Downsmen, the pond is lined with a layer of impervious clay and relies on water condensing from the cool night air to keep it topped up with water.

## Steyning
*Map 2 ref H6*

*10 miles SE of Billingshurst off the A283*

Now a prosperous small country town, Steyning was founded in the 8th century by St Cuthman who, according to local legend, settled here as a boy after the cart in which he was pushing his invalid mother broke down on a journey from the West Country. St Cuthman went on to build a timber church in which Ethelwulf, father of King Alfred, is believed to have been buried. In the 12th century, the Saxon structure was replaced by the fine Romanesque church of St Andrew, which at one time was part of a larger monastic house belonging to the abbey at Fecamp in Normandy. Despite its unexceptional outward appearance, the building has a striking interior with towering Norman columns, a 12th century marble font and some impressive carved stonework.

By the late Saxon period, Steyning had grown to become an important port on the then navigable estuary of the River Adur, but around 1100, the silting up of the river forced the quay to close. However, the community had become sufficiently established by then to sustain itself as a small market town; many of the fine late medieval buildings which survive in High and Church Streets were constructed in a variety of styles and materials in the centuries which followed.

Indeed, Steyning is filled with exceptional examples of early domestic buildings, and is home to 125 listed buildings. There are examples of several 14th and 15th century 'hall' type houses, such as the **Post Office** and **Penfold Cottage**, and 'Wealden' cottages, such as **Workhouse Cottage** in Mouse Lane. Another outstanding structure is Steyning's famous **Old Grammar School** which was founded in 1614 in a long timber-framed building in Church Street; this has a characteristic overhanging upper storey and a roof covered with thin slabs of Horsham stone, and is now used as a school library. A good place to discover more about the town's long and eventful history is the **Steyning Museum** in Church Street.

Steyning's close proximity to the South Downs Way and the Downs Link, the long-distance bridleway which follows the course of the old railway line to Christ's Hospital near Horsham and on to Guildford, makes this lovely village an excellent base for walking and riding holidays. The same can be said of Bramber, the former

Norman administrative centre and garrison town which lies beside the Adur, one mile to the east.

### Bramber
*Map 2 ref H7*
*11 miles SE of Billingshurst off the A283*

Following the Norman Invasion, William the Conqueror granted the land at Bramber to his trusted lieutenant, William de Braose, who erected a wooden keep on top of a prominent chalky outcrop beside the river. Around 1070 the timber structure was replaced by stone fortifications which included a gatehouse and a number of domestic buildings surrounded by a curtain wall - ***Bramber Castle*** became an important stronghold which was visited by, among others, King John and Edward I; however, the town's subsequent decline and the effects of Parliamentarian cannon-fire reduced most of the castle to rubble except for the conspicuous 75 foot high section of the gatehouse keep which can be seen today. William de Braose was also responsible for building the chapel at the foot of the castle mound in 1075, now the parish church of St Nicholas. Despite a number of major alterations throughout the centuries, the original nave and church tower remain.

In the 15th century the lands of the de Braose family were transferred to Magdalen College, Oxford, whose founder, William Wayneflete, the then Bishop of Winchester, constructed the striking mediaeval residence in Bramber known as ***St Mary's*** in 1470. This Grade I listed building, with its classic half-timbered Wealden facade, has a fine wood-panelled room with Elizabethan trompe l'oeil painting and mediaeval shuttered windows. Originally built as a monastic hospital to serve pilgrims en route along the South Downs Way to Canterbury, it was at one time inhabited by the monastic wardens of the adjacent bridge over the River Adur, a structure which until the 1470s had an unusual chapel at its centre. The King's Room is believed to have been Charles II's last sleeping-place on his flight from the Battle of Worcester before he embarked for the ship waiting to take him from Shoreham to safe exile in France. Recently restored, today's visitors to St Mary's can view the magnificent interior and exterior, including the topiary garden, before enjoying homemade refreshments in the music room.

Before the Reform Act of 1832 swept away the so called rotten boroughs, the tiny constituencies of Bramber, Steyning and Shoreham each returned two MPs to Westminster. This was in spite of the fact that at one time Bramber had only 32 eligible voters. One MP who benefited from the unreformed system was William

Wilberforce, who was more or less 'awarded' one of the Bramber seats in recognition for his campaigning work against slavery and social injustice; he is said to have made only one fleeting visit to his constituency during the whole of his 12 year tenure.

## Findon                                                     *Map 2 ref G7*
*12 miles SE of Billingshurst off the A24*

Findon is a village within the South Downs Area of Outstanding Natural Beauty close to Worthing and yet only four miles from the sea. This attractive village is centred round an elegant square containing a 17th century inn and some fine 18th century residential buildings. The flint-built village church of St John the Baptist stands on the opposite side of the main road; despite having been heavily restored by Sir George Gilbert Scott in the 1870s, it contains some interesting early features, including a 13th century oak screen and a mediaeval font fashioned from Sussex marble which is shaped like a cattle trough (a more dainty 19th century replacement stands nearby). Set within attractive wooded grounds a few yards from the church is **Findon Place**, an early 18th century mansion which was enlarged later in the century.

Findon is perhaps most famous for being the venue for one of the two great Sussex sheep fairs (the other is at Lewes), an annual event which takes place on the second Saturday in September. A market on Nepcote Green has been held since the 13th century; each year the village takes on a festival atmosphere, and as well as around 20,000 sheep changing hands, there are a great many additional activities and attractions which people come from miles around to enjoy. At one time, there were three farriers' workshops in the village, reflecting Findon's other long tradition as a horse-training centre.

Findon is also the access point for the large Iron Age hill fort of **Cissbury Ring**, two and a half miles to the south of Chanctonbury. Overshadowed only by Dorset's Maiden Castle, this impressive hilltop site covers an area of 65 acres and is surrounded by a double rampart almost a mile in circumference. It has been estimated that over 50,000 tons of chalk soil and boulders would have had to be moved in its construction, a feat which was carried out in the 3rd century BC and would have required a sizeable Iron Age community. Cissbury was occupied for around two centuries before it was allowed to revert to pastureland; however, the threat of a Saxon invasion following the departure of the Romans led to reoccupation and a major strengthening of the earthwork ramparts. Today,

Cissbury Ring is owned by the National Trust and is open to the public free of charge.

### High Salvington
*Map 2 ref G7*
*12 miles SE of Billingshurst off the A24*

High Salvington is the site of the mganificently restored **Salvington Windmill**, which dates back to the beginning of the18th century. It is described as a post mill, a type which was in common use from the late mediaeval period and consists of a heavy cross-shaped base with a strong central upright around which the windmill's sails and timber superstructure were able to pivot.

A couple of miles further west, the A27 passes to the north of the cone-shaped **Highdown Hill** which, although only 266 feet high, stands out above the surrounding coastal plain. Its prominent nature has led to a long history of occupation and, in its time, it has been an Iron Age hill fort, a Roman bathhouse and a Saxon graveyard (relics from these different eras are on view in Worthing Museum.) The white-painted country house known as **Castle Goring** stands on the northern side of Highdown Hill; this exceptional residence was built in Italian style for the grandfather of the poet, Percy Bysshe Shelley.

### Patching
*Map 2 ref G7*
*13 miles SE of Billingshurst off the A280*

The attractive village of Patching, close to Littlehampton, Arundel and Worthing and not far from the Wetland Centre off the A280, is home to **The Fox**, a distinguished and impressive public house where visitors can enjoy real ales and excellent food. The strikingly hand-

**The Fox**

some red and white exterior is an indication of this pub's distinction and traditional ambience. A well kept, family run establishment owned by three chefs, this supremely comfortable free house boasts a large L-shaped bar and open fires, and is just the place to enjoy King Barnes ales and hearty home-cooked meals. The extensive and lovely two acres of garden are peaceful and relaxing; from here it is only a short walk to lovely woods, and also quite close the South Downs. The atmosphere is welcoming and friendly as well as quiet and restful. Meals available all day, from 11 a.m. til 11 p.m., as there is always a chef in residence! *The Fox, Arundel Road, Patching, West Sussex BN13 3UJ Tel: 01903 871337.*

# Arundel

A settlement since pre-Roman times, Arundel stands at the strategically important point where the major east-west land route through Sussex crosses the River Arun. One of William the Conqueror's most favoured knights, Roger de Montgomery, first built a **castle** on the high ground above the river. This was similar to the castle at Windsor in that it consisted of a motte and double bailey, a plan which, despite several alterations to the fabric of the building, remains largely unaltered to this day.

The period of stability the castle brought to the town in the late medieval period made Arundel into an important port and market town. It was during this era that the 14th century parish church of St Nicholas was built, a unique building in that it is now divided into separate Catholic and Anglican areas by a Sussex iron screen. The Fitzalan Chapel in the choir houses the tombs of the Catholic Earls of Arundel and Dukes of Norfolk, in whose family the castle has remained for the past 500 years; entry to this section can normally only be made through the castle grounds.

During the English Civil War, Parliamentarian forces bombarded the castle using cannons fired from the church tower. This bombardment led to the destruction of most of the Norman fortifications, the only parts to survive being the 12th century shell keep on the central mound and parts of the 13th century barbican and curtain wall. The rest of the structure remained in ruins until a programme of restoration during the 1790s made the castle habitable once again. (One of the finest rooms in Arundel Castle, the mahogany lined library, dates from this period.) A second restoration, amounting to a virtual rebuilding, was carried out about 100 years later by

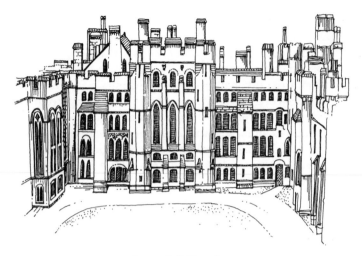

*Arundel Castle*

the 15th Duke, funded by profits from the family's ownership of the newly prosperous steel town of Sheffield.

Most of the colossal structure which can be seen today is therefore a 19th century Gothic reproduction. However, the state apartments and main rooms contain some fine period furniture dating from the 16th century, a fine collection of tapestries, and paintings by such artists as Reynolds, Van Dyck, Gainsborough, Holbein and Constable. The nearby 1,000 acre Arundel Castle grounds are also open to the public.(Please note that the castle is closed during the winter months.)

Despite religious persecution, particularly during the 16th century, the Fitzalan family and the successive Dukes of Norfolk remained staunchly Roman Catholic. The 15th Duke, who was responsible for the 19th century rebuilding of the castle, also commissioned the substantial Catholic church of St Philip Neri which was designed in French Gothic style by J A Hansom and Son, the inventors of the Hansom cab, in 1870. In 1965, this impressive building became the seat of the Catholic bishopric of Brighton and Arundel, and was renamed the *Cathedral of Our Lady and St Philip Howard.* (St Philip Howard was the 13th Earl of Arundel who died in prison after being sentenced to death by Elizabeth I for his Catholic beliefs; his remains are now in the cathedral, along with an impressive memorial shrine.) Each June, the cathedral hosts the two-day Corpus Christ Festival during which the entire length of the aisle is laid out with a carpet of fresh flowers.

Situated in quiet Tarrant Square off Tarrant Street in central Arundel, the gift shop *Crystal Clear* offers a range of unusual and delightful gift ideas. The shop specialises, as the name suggests, in beautiful crystals of all kinds, each one unique, including rough hewn rock crystals in many striking shades and finely delicate Austrian crystals. The accent is definitely on the New Age, as a glance inside the attractive shopfront reveals: a wide variety of aromatherapy oils, oil burners, natural Bach flower remedies, incense, candles, rain sticks, relaxation cassette tapes, and specialist cards to use for tarot, astrology and runes readings are available. A selection of cards,

*Crystal Clear*

books on New Age subjects and gifts such as picture frames, gift baskets, oil lamps, glassware and glass and crystal ornaments completes the esoteric experience to be had in this singular and charming shop. Proprietor Debbie Hayers and her staff are on hand with friendly and courteous help and service. *Crystal Clear, 3, Tarrant Square, Tarrant Street, Arundel, West Sussex BN18 9DE*

Other historic sites in Arundel include the *Maison Dieu*, a medieval hospital which can be found outside the Mill Road lodge of Arundel Castle. Founded in 1345 by Richard Fitzalan and dissolved by Henry VIII in 1546, this semi-monastic institution combined the roles of clinic, hotel and almshouse. The heart of the old town contains some fine Georgian and Victorian houses and inns, most notably in Maltravers and Tarrant Streets. The parish chuch dates from the 14th century.

In a handsome row of shops in quiet Tarrant Street, Arundel, *Country Bunches* stands apart for the abundance and elegance of its wares. This charming gift shop offers a wealth of tasteful and original gift ideas. Apart from the excellent assortment of artificial flowers, this very pretty establishment offers a delightful array of delicate porcelain dolls, dainty china cherubs, angels and other figurines, several picnics' worth of Teddy bears (in all shapes and sizes), decorative glassware, hand-made and unique birthday and christmas cards, and many other attractive collectibles. The proprietors, Barry and Vera Cookman, create many of the gifts themselves, and their craftsmanship and artistry are evident. The shop also features a fine range of period Victorian lighting and, on the recently refurbished second floor, mirrors in a selection of unusual and highly decorative styles. This superior shop is a must for

*Country Bunches*

anyone looking for a truly special gift. *Country Bunches, 4 Tarrant Street, Arundel, West Sussex BN18 9DG  Tel: 01903 883073*

Arundel also contains a couple of interesting museums; the privately-owned *Arundel Toy and Military Museum* is located in a charming Georgian cottage in the High Street known as the Doll's House. Inside, visitors can see a unique collection of antique dolls, teddy bears, puppets, games, boats, tin toys and around 3,000 toy soldiers. Further along the High Street, the *Arundel Museum and Heritage Centre* gives an fascinating insight into the people and activities of the town through imaginative use of models, old photographs and historic artefacts.

David and Susan Haines have recently acquired the 19th century *Arundel Park Hotel*, a welcoming and attractive hotel and pub within walking distance of the many attractions of lovely Arundel Castle and town centre. Your very friendly and gregarious hosts go out of their way to ensure that all of their guests feel at home. Though large and impressive, this fine establishment manages at the same time to be both homely and extremely comfortable. David and Susan have brought their boundless enthusiasm to refurbishing the premises, so that the 11 good-sized guest bedrooms have been tastefully redecorated while retaining their original charm and cosiness.

*The Arundel Park Hotel*

Within minutes of the railway station, this Free House offers real ales on tap and excellent meals - good hearty English fare is the byword here. The ambience in the bar is congenial and warm, and there is also an outdoor beer garden - just the place for a quiet pint in relaxing, scenic surroundings. *Arundel Park Hotel, Station Road, The Causeway, Arundel, West Sussex BN18 9JL Tel: 01903 882588 Fax: 01903 883808*

Another good place to visit lies about two miles north of Arundel on the A284 road to Offham and South Stoke. The 60 acre woodland site run by the **Wildfowl and Wetlands Trust** contains a wide variety of ducks, geese, swans and other wildfowl from all over the world. Many of the birds can be viewed at close quarters, with Arundel Castle providing a dramatic backdrop. There is also an award-winning visitor centre with a viewing gallery, gift shop and restaurant.

**Offham House** was originally built for the Duke of Norfolk's mother, and retains the richness and splendour of a bygone age. Now an elegant bed and breakfast, this beautiful and impressive house is located in the peaceful hamlet of Offham, along the River Arun. The handsome, very large rooms are tastefully decorated

**Offham House**

and furnished with pieces that are in keeping with the period of the house. The view from the rooms takes in the lovely, secluded gardens and surrounding countryside - perfect for long walks and birdwatching. This genteel B&B makes a good base for exploring picturesque Offham and, of course, Arundel itself, just a few miles away - a treasure trove of antiques shops and other pleasant diversions. Owner Sally Spanner makes every effort to ensure her guests' comfort and convenience, and takes justified pride in this delightfully hidden-away house, which offers comfortable and distinguished accommodation that will suit the most discerning visitor. *Offham House, Near Arundel, West Sussex BN18 9PD Tel: 01903 882129; 0860 901596*

## Burpham                                        *Map 2 ref F7*
*1 mile NE of Arundel off the A284*

Another impressive view of Arundel Castle can be enjoyed from the peaceful, picturesque and unspoilt village of Burpham. This small and peaceful settlement lies across the river from the Wildfowl Trust, but can only be reached along a narrow three mile cul-de-sac which leads up from the A27 along the eastern bank of the Arun. Burpham consists of an attractive collection of flint and brick-built thatched cottages, with a pleasant 18th century inn, century old cricket ground and a sizable Norman church. This historic church was built in the 12th and 13th centuries, mainly of flint but with the occasional inclusion of rubble from a Roman structure which once stood on the site (sections of a Roman pavement have since been discovered in the north transept). During the Middle Ages, a remote farm on nearby Wepham Down was the site of a leper colony; the track leading down to the village from the Downs is still known as Lepers' Way. The walks around Burpham are truly spectacular.

Nearly at the end of a 2½ mile cul de sac, signposted for Burpham, which turns off the A27 almost alongside Arundel Railway Station, you will find *The Burpham Country House Hotel*, the ideal place to get away from it all and take a *'Stress-Remedy Break'*. Parts of this picturesque old house date back to 1710. Reputed to have once been a hunting lodge for the Duke of Norfolk, today it is owned by George and Marianne Walker; together they have built up a fine

*The Burpham Country House Hotel*

reputation for offering first-class accommodation, cuisine and service. Rapidly being acknowledged as one of West Sussex's top dining venues, chef Marianne, who is Swiss, recently won a well deserved AA rosette for culinary excellence. All the dishes on her ever changing menu are prepared using only the best ingredients and can be accompanied by a fine wine from the extensive wine list. The hotel also has its own cocktail lounge bar, where you can relax on comfortable sofas in front of an open fire while enjoying a quiet pre-dinner drink. Most of the bedrooms enjoy lovely views of the South Downs; all have en-suite facilities and, as you would expect from a hotel of this calibre, are exquisitely furnished and superbly equipped. ETB 3 Crowns Highly Recommended. AA 2 Star 75% and Rosette,

Johansens Recommended. *The Burpham Country House Hotel, Burpham, Nr Arundel, West Sussex B18 9RJ Tel: 01903 882160. Fax: 01903 884627*

## Walberton
*Map 1 ref E7*

*3 miles W of Arundel off the A27*

This handsome village is home to **Beam Ends**, a delightful, traditional tearoom occupying a charming 16th century thatched cottage. From the tea garden guests can enjoy scenic views across open countryside as they tuck into the range of delicious lunches and snacks available, all home-made by owner Coral Botteley (ably assisted by husband Rick). The cream teas are a special treat: home-made scones and a choice of six different loose leaf teas. The lunch

**Beam Ends**

menu is based on typical English fare such as cottage pie, fish cakes, apple pie and Bakewell tart and always includes a vegetarian dish; a full roast lunch is available on Sundays (booking advisable). Locally supplied quality teas, stoneground flour and home-made preserves are also available to buy. As an added treat, motoring enthusiasts can marvel at Rick's choice collection of classic and vintage motor cars. And if you decide you'd like to stay in the area for a bit longer, B&B accommodation is available in the cottage itself. Open: May to September, Tuesday to Saturday 11 a.m. to 5.30 p.m. October to April restricted opening; please call to check hours. *'Beam Ends', Hedgers Hill, Walberton, Arundel, West Sussex BN18 0LR Tel: 01243 551254*

## Slindon
*Map 1 ref E7*
*4 miles W of Arundel off the A29*

The picturesque village of Slindon stands on a shelf of the South Downs. In a nearby beech wood there is a shingle beach, evidence that the seashore once was situated here instead of five miles away to the south. With its views across the coastal plain to the English Channel, this excellent observation point has been occupied since Neolithic times; many fine examples of early flint tools having been found in the locality. The village, whose name is derived from the Saxon word for sloping hill, is arranged as a loose square of narrow lanes, the focal point of which is a crossroads at the northwestern corner where a tree stands in small open area near the *church*. Dating from the 12th century, this charming flint built church contains an unusual reclining effigy of a Tudor knight, Sir Anthony St Leger, the only wooden carving of its kind in Sussex.

**Slindon House** was founded as a residence for the Archbishops of Canterbury. (Archbishop Stephen Langton, a negotiator and signatory of the Magna Carta, spent the last weeks of his life here in 1228.) Rebuilt in the 1560s and extensively remodelled during the 1920s, the house is now a private boys' school. Slindon's wonderful post office is an amalgamation of two 400 year old cottages and is the village's only remaining thatched building. Just to the north of the village, there is a cricket field where Sir Richard Newland is said to have refined the modern game over 200 years ago. The public footpath that runs nearby offers lovely views across Littlehampton to the sea and makes a pleasant stroll to the local pub.

This exceptionally attractive settlement of redbrick and flint cottages also forms part of the 3,500 acre **Slindon Park Woodlands**, the largest National Trust owned estate in Sussex, offering excellent opportunities for walking and birdwatching.

To the north, the Slindon Estate is bordered by Stane Street, the Roman road which once ran from Chichester to London. The remains of the Roman pavement, which was constructed (complete with sophisticated drainage ditches) almost 2,000 years ago, lie a foot beneath the surface of the present day bridleway. The three and a half mile stretch through Eartham Wood and on to Bignor Hill is unusually well preserved, perhaps because for centuries the local community knew it as the *'Devil's Road'* and left it well alone.

## Eartham
*Map 1 ref D7*
*6 miles NW of Arundel off the A27*

From Slindon village there is a marvellous circular walk around the Slindon Estate which takes in Slindon Folly, a lonely flint archway built in 1817, and the village of Eartham, the former home of the 19th century MP William Huskisson. Huskisson was knocked down by Stevenson's Rocket during its inaugural run in 1830, earning him the doubtful honour of being the world's first recorded victim of a railway accident. Within a mile of the South Downs Way at the northern end of Slindon Estate, the National Trust has recently opened *Gumber Bothy*, a traditional farm building which has been converted to provide basic accommodation and cooking facilities for up to 27 people.

## *Fontwell*                                                     *Map 1 ref D7*
*5 miles W of Arundel off the A27*

Fontwell is home to the pleasantly situated *Fontwell Park National Hunt* racecourse. Horse racing has taken place here since 1921. The 'figure of eight' jumping course holds 15 fixtures each season and attracts a large following of show-jumping enthusiasts. The delightful three and a half acre **Denman's Garden** can be found close by; this beautifully sheltered semi-wild garden welcomes visitors and has a section offering a good range of homegrown plants.

# CHAPTER THREE
## The West Sussex Weald

*Leonardslee Gardens, Lower Beeding*

# Chapter 3 - Area Covered

*For precise location of places please refer to the colour maps found at the rear of the book.*

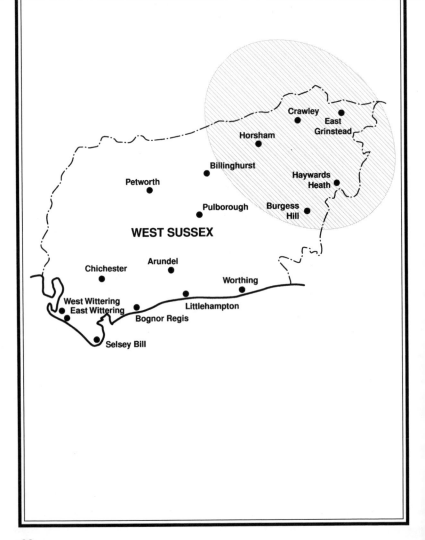

# 3
# *The West Sussex Weald*

## Introduction

The area to the north of the South Downs is called the Weald, a word related to the German word *Wald*, or forest. This suggests an area covered in woodland; though the tree cover is still quite extensive, pastures enclosed by hedgerows are the dominant feature of this part of central West Sussex. The two outlying flanks of chalk Downs to the north and south are the remnants of a great chalk dome which once covered southern England; Wealden clays cover the low levels between these hill ridges. As might be expected, the Wealden landscape is complicated and varied, a patchwork of hedge-lined pastures, small woodlands and the stretches of heathy ground.

Traditional Wealden buildings can be found throughout the region: timber-framed and hung with pantiles. The distinctive 'hall houses' are also a feature of this area: timber-framed with hefty Horsham 'slate' roofs, popular in the 15th and 16th centuries - one fine example is Priest House in West Hoathly. The area is also rich in stately homes such as Standen in Worth, and wonderful gardens such as Nymans, Leonardslee and Borde Hill.

Historic Horsham, West and East Grinstead and Crawley are the region's main towns. The local villages are renowned for their beauty, tranquillity, history and traditional charm.

## Horsham

The historic town of Horsham, which takes its name from a Saxon term meaning *horse pasture*, was founded in the mid 10th century.

By the 13th century, Horsham had grown into a prosperous borough and market town which was considered sufficiently important to send two members to the new Parliament established in 1295.

Between 1306 and 1830, Horsham took it in turns with Lewes and Chichester to hold the county assizes. During the weeks the court was in session, large numbers of outsiders were attracted into the town, which would take on something of a carnival atmosphere. Public executions were sometimes carried out on Horsham Common or at the Carfax (today a thriving pedestrianized shopping area),

*Horsham*

including one in 1735 of a man who refused to speak at his trial and was subjected to 'death by compression'. Three hundred weight of stones were placed on his chest for three days. When he still refused to speak the goaler added his own weight, killing the man outright. The last such execution of its kind in England took place in Horsham in 1844. During the 17th century, Horsham's county gaol was also used to accommodate members of the much persecuted Society of Friends.

The old part of Horsham consists of a long wedge shaped former green, with the part-Norman 12th century *Church of St Mary* at one end. Stretching between the two is a unique walkway known as

***The Causeway***; approached down a narrow passage called Pump Alley. Many of the town's finest buildings are located in the Causeway, including the town hall with its facade built by the Duke of Norfolk in 1812, the Manor House, headquarters of the RSPCA, and the 15th century King's Head Hotel. One of the finest examples of a timber-framed Sussex town house can be seen at 30 The Causeway, whilst at No. 9, the Tudor built Causeway House is the location of the impressive ***Horsham Museum***.

This is a treasure trove of exhibits and artefacts covering local history and a wealth of interests ranging from town and country pursuits to 19th century literature. The expression of over 100 years of collecting, this fine museum is located in a timber-framed former merchant's house dating back to the 15th century. The museum occupies two floors: on the ground floor is the Tourist Information Centre along with the museum's row of reconstructed 19th century emporia including a cycle shop, saddlery and chemist's, as well as rooms devoted to Sussex iron and glass, temporary exhibitions and the local trades gallery, highlighting the work of the town's artisans.

***The Horsham Museum***

The exhibits on the first floor focus on social history and the history of Horsham itself, featuring domestic crafts, as well as a special room devoted to the poet Percy Bysshe Shelley (born and bred 2 miles away), a costume display, a room devoted to flints and fossils (including some dinosaur bones!) and displays of curiosities garnered from all over the region. All this and a delightful walled garden. The museum is open Monday to Saturday, 10 a.m. to 5 p.m. Admission free. *Horsham Museum, 9 The Causeway, Horsham, West Sussex RH12 1HE Tel: 01403 254959.*

Two miles southwest of Horsham, the famous **Christ's Hospital**, a Bluecoat School, lies in the heart of the Sussex countryside. Founded in London in 1552 by Edward VI, the school moved to Horsham in 1902; the present buildings incorporate some of the original London edifices. 'Bluecoat' refers to the traditional long dark blue cloak and girdle still worn by the 800 or so pupils, both boys and girls. The school has a strong academic and artistic reputation, and incorporates an arts complex and a refectory where a famous painting by Antonio Verrio is on permanent display. Visitors' guided tours are available by arrangement.

# Around Horsham

### Broadbridge Heath
*Map 3 ref G3*

2 miles W of Horsham off the A24/A281

The handsome village of Broadbridge Heath boasts the distinctive modern **Church of St John** and the Shelley C P school, named after the poet, who was born at Field Place, on the edge of the village. His grandfather lived at Arun House in Horsham.

**The Shelley Arms** is a grand and very attractive Tudor style public house in the village of Broadbridge Heath, offering good food

**The Shelley Arms**

and real ales.Originally thought to date back only to the 19th century, it was only when the parish council set about earmarking buildings of possible historical interest that the truth emerged: parts of the main building date back to Elizabethan times. There has been a house, probably at first a small farmhouse or homestead, on the site since before 1600. A document dated 1834 outlines a lease agreement between Sir Timothy Shelley and one Richard Hardling; Shelley family ownership ceased in 1898. This is a pub that has grown over the years, the additions cleverly added on. The spruce interior boasts exposed beams, wood panelling and is very pleasant, peaceful and relaxed. Proprietors Malcolm Parker and Kim Chapman and their friendly, helpful staff make every effort to ensure that visitors have an enjoyable and relaxing time. *The Shelley Arms, 16 Old Guildford Road, Broadbridge Heath, Horsham, West Sussex RH12 3JU Tel: 01403 253406.*

## Warnham                                                 *Map 2 ref H3*
2 miles NW of Horsham off the A24

Warnham is a diverse community which lies scattered between the A29 and A24 trunk routes. The buildings here vary from a modern brickworks to some fine old residences, including **Warnham Court**, the home of the Lucas family. **Field Place** on the edge of Warnham was the birthplace of the poet Percy Bysshe Shelley in 1792. After a reasonably happy childhood, which included exploring the local countryside, boating on Warnham's millpond (now part of **Warnham Nature Reserve**) and St Leonards Forest, Shelley was cast out of his family home by his father, who didn't approve of his son's chosen profession. The gardens of Field Place are open to visitors for a few days each year .

## Kingsfold                                               *Map 2 ref H2*
*3 miles N of Horsham off the A24*

Set in bucolic splendour in the West Sussex village of Kingsfold, ¼ mile north of A24/A29 junction not far from Horsham, is **Wattlehurst Farm,** an open farm comprising 50 acres of land given over to various uses. This welcoming establishment is home to a veritable menagerie of animals including llamas, pygmy goats, wallabies, potbelly pigs, chicks, bantams, ducks, ponies, fallow deer, sheep, lambs, rabbits and guinea pigs. All the animals can be petted, including new lambs during lambing season. The farm also boasts a small museum and lovely nature trail. The small purpose built cafe located in the barn area serves hot and cold drinks, ice-creams, sandwiches, cakes and other snacks. Souvenirs on sale include badges,

**Wattlehurst Farm**

pins and other memorabilia. Owner Brian Betchley and manager Stephanie Mann, having recently acquired this established concern, open their doors to educational group tours, birthday parties, and corporate days out at the extensive trout lake. Open to the public Sundays 10-5 in summer; 10.30-4.30 in winter. *Wattlehurst Farm, Kingsfold, Horsham, West Sussex RH12 3SD  Tel: 01306 627490.*

### Rusper                                                   *Map 2 ref H2*
4 miles N of Horsham off the A24

Rusper is a fine old monastic village. While in the area, you might want to stop for some refreshment at ***The Royal Oak***, just outside Rusper. Once the smallest pub in Sussex, this delightful bolthole is

**The Royal Oak**

a true country pub, hardly altered by time. The former blacksmith's next door was converted a few years back and annexed to the original building, which retains its traditional air of elegance and comfort.The beamed ceilings and large open fires attest to this particular Oak's 18th century roots. As this is a King Barnes Sussex beer house, run by Dave and Jean Tilbey, a range of real ales is on offer. All the food is home-prepared and home-cooked - the bubble and squeak is a tasty favourite, and the savoury steak and kidney pie, steaks, chicken and other traditional dishes on the menu are worth the visit alone. The ambience is friendly, cosy and quiet; visitors can relax in front of the log fires in winter and in the lovely garden on warmer days. *The Royal Oak, Friday Street, Rusper, West Sussex RH12 4QA Tel: 01293 871393.*

## *Itchingfield* *Map 2 ref G3*
*2 miles SW of Horsham off the A24/A264*

Just outside the village of Itchingfield, between Horsham and Billingshurst, ***Woodpeckers*** is a pretty country cottage offering bed and breakfast accommodation. Set in a quiet country lane, this delightful establishment is brimming with charm. Owner Gill Peskett is a very pleasant, conscientious host who has taken great pains to decorate and furnish each of the three spacious guest bedrooms to

***Woodpeckers***

the highest standards of taste and comfort. Guests have use of a lounge and dining room, and are welcome to stroll and relax in the lovely 1 1/2 acre garden, at times visited by deer, rabbits and many species of birds.

Local places of interest, apart from the charming village which has a 12th century church, include the famous Causeway in Horsham, with houses dating back to the 14th century, cobbled streets and gas lamps, not forgetting a superb shopping centre. Woodpeckers is surrounded by good walking country which includes the Downs Link running from Shoreham on the South Downs to Guildford on the North Downs. Woodpeckers is ideally situated midway between the coast (22 miles) and London (just 55 minutes by train). Visit once and you may find yourself among the many guests who return again and again. *Woodpeckers, Bashurst Hill, Itchingfield, Horsham, West Sussex RH13 7NY Tel: 01403 790228.*

## Handcross                                         *Map 2 ref I3*
*3 miles E of Horsham off the A279*

Handcross is home of the celebrated National Trust-owned **Nymans Garden**. Set around the ruins of a country mansion, this splendid 30 acre landscaped area is one of the great gardens of the Sussex Weald, with rare and beautiful plants collected from all corners of the world. The walled garden, with its fountain, the hidden sunken garden, old rose garden, topiary garden, laurel walk, pinetum and woodland walks make Nymans a delight all year round. Together, these contain a wonderful collection of specimen trees, shrubs and flowering plants, many of which are native to other continents. In 1997, a few rooms in Nymans house were opened to the public for the first time, affording insight into the family who first created this extraordinary garden.

Another natural beauty in Handcross is **High Beeches Gardens Conservation Trust** - 20 acres of wonderful landscaped woodland and water gardens.

## Lower Beeding                                     *Map 2 ref I4*
*3 miles SE of Horsham off the A279*

A distinctive hammer pond can be found just to the north of Lower Beeding on the southern fringe of **St Leonards Forest**. This 10,000 acre wooded heath is one of the few treed areas to survive the long-term ravages of the timber fuelled iron industry. Rising in places to around 500 feet, the forest lies on the undulating sandstone ridge bounded by Horsham, Crawley and Handcross. According to local folklore, St Leonards Forest is the home of a legendary nine foot dragon which roamed the heath and terrorised the surrounding villagers. Coincidentally, the bones of a prehistoric iguanodon have since been discovered in the Forest by the Sussex-based geologist, Dr Gideon Mantell.

## *Crabtree*

*Map 2 ref I4*

*4 miles SE of Horsham off the A281*

The beautiful **Leonardslee Gardens** lie in a natural valley on the eastern side of the A281, between Lower Beeding and the village of Crabtree. Laid out in the early 19th century, this spectacular spring-flowering landscape garden in a peaceful 240 acre valley with seven

**Leonardslee Gardens**

beautiful lakes has been extensively planted with rhododendrons, azaleas, magnolias and other specimen shrubs. There's an interesting summer wildflower walk, rock garden, marvellous bonsai exhibition and alpine house. Deer and wallabies live in semi-wild conditions around the series of small lakes, which may have been former hammer ponds. Also on site is a collection of Victorian motorcars, a licensed restaurant, cafe, giftshop and plants for sale.

## *Cowfold*

*Map 2 ref I5*

*5 miles SE of Horsham off the A281*

Cowfold's parish **Church of St Peter** is surrounded by some charming domestic buildings and contains an exceptional 15th century monumental brass of the prior of St Pancras Priory in Lewes; this renowned monastic house belonged to the rare Cluniac order and was home to the talented team of artists who, a couple of centuries earlier, were responsible for painting some of the most exceptional ecclesiastical murals in Sussex.

It is hard to believe today that Cowfold was once an important centre of the iron industry. The abundance of timber for fuel and reliable streams to drive the bellows and heavy hammers made this an active iron-smelting area from mediaeval times to the end of the 18th century. In order to secure a steady supply of water to these early foundries, small rivers were dammed to form triangular mill or hammer ponds; a number of disused examples can still be seen in the surrounding woodlands, especially around Crabtree, a couple of miles to the north.

### West Grinstead                                   *Map 2 ref H5*
*6 miles S of Horsham off the A24*

West Grinstead is a somewhat scattered community with a fine country house and two interesting churches: designed in the early 1800s by the famous Regency architect John Nash, **West Grinstead Park** is now an established racehorse breeding centre which is part of the National Stud. The parish church of St George dates from early Norman times and has an unusual 15th century timbered porch; the stability of early 19th century life in this part of rural Sussex is reflected in the names of the local farms which can still be seen painted on the backs of the church pews. A long-established centre of Catholicism, West Grinstead also possesses a Catholic church which was regularly visited by the writer Hilaire Belloc when he was resident at nearby Shipley.

One mile to the west of West Grinstead, the busy A24 runs alongside the stark ruin of **Knepp Castle**, the fortification built by William de Braose of Bramber to defend the upper reaches of the River Adur. All that remains of this once impressive Norman keep is a solitary wall standing on top of a low earthwork mound, or motte, which in turn is surrounded by a dry moat. The rest of the castle was demolished in 1726 and the rubble used to form the base for a new road between Horsham and Steyning, above which motorists still travel today.

### Dial Post                                        *Map 2 ref H5*
*6 miles S of Horsham off the A24*

Here in the charming village of Dial Post, within easy distance of West Grinstead and Henfield and convenient for the south coast resorts of Worthing, Littlehampton and Shoreham-by-Sea, **Honeybridge Park** is a handsome and picturesque caravan park in a lovely countryside setting boasting excellent views and very

*Honeybridge Park*

good facilities. Located down quiet, rural Honeybridge Lane, this pleasant and spotless site is ideal for a quiet, relaxing holiday. Owners Valerie and Jeff Burrows have recently acquired the site and are working hard to offer more and more conveniences while maintaining the site's secluded and uncrowded atmosphere. The handy on-site shop is well stocked, and there is good access to and from the site. Enjoying a central location with marvellous views over idyllic countryside, Honeybridge Park makes for an ideal family holiday - children can play in perfect safety as the site is in a country lane with very little through traffic - or for anyone looking to get away from it all and enjoy some truly pastoral surroundings. *Honeybridge Park, Honeybridge Lane, Dial Post, West Sussex RH13 8NX Tel: 01403 710923.*

## Coolham
*Map 2 ref G4*

*5 miles S of Horsham on the A272*

**The Blue Idol Guest House** is set at the end of a long lane in an old apple orchard. Dating back to the reign of Elizabeth I and established as a Quaker Meeting House in 1691, when the original 16th century farmhouse was converted by William Penn - founder of the US state of Pennsylvania - and other Quakers, this beautiful clapboard and whitewashed stone building with its timbered walls and Horsham stone roof offers peaceful and homely accommodation. Regardless of your faith, the quiet serenity of the adjacent Meeting Room inspires thought, repose and meditation.

Although obviously a place of religious significance, this will not impinge upon your stay; when queried, proprietors Julie and

**The Blue Idol Quaker Guesthouse**

Jonathan Spencer are happy to discuss their uniquely quiet and spiritual faith. The gardens are a haven of peace and tranquillity, the rooms furnished simply and comfortably in the Quaker way, with handsome washstands and basins in every room. Guests are assured a warm welcome from Julie and Jonathan and their two young children. Non smoking. *The Blue Idol Quaker Guesthouse, Old House Lane, Coolham, Horsham, West Sussex RH13 8QP  Tel: 01403 741241  Fax: 01403 741841 email: 106700.3252@compuserve.com*

## Henfield                                                    *Map 2 ref I6*
*9 miles S of Horsham off the A281*

Henfield was once an important staging post on the busy London to Brighton coaching route. The village contains a couple of good former coaching inns, a much restored church built on Saxon foundations, and an eccentric 16th century cottage known as the **Cat House** which is decorated with a collection of highly unusual iron cats. These were made by local joiner Bob Ward to scare off the vicar's cat after it had crept in and eaten his pet canary. **The Henfield Village Museum** in the village hall contains an interesting collection of historic artefacts including agricultural tools, costumes, local paintings and photographs, illustrating life in a rural area from medieval times to the present day.

**The White Hart** is a place to be at home in. Nestling on a picturesque village High street, just 10 minutes from the South Downs and Devil's Dyke, and two minutes from Henfield Museum and the famous Henfield Cat House, its clientele are a happy blend of locals and visitors, giving the place an excellent community feel for both young and old. There is evidence that the stately and impressive brick-built building dates back to the 13th century, and was once a coaching house and smugglers' retreat. The interior is enhanced by two inglenook fireplaces, and many original rafters are in evidence. All the food on offer in the restaurant and at the bar is home-cooked, and there is an extensive and varied choice of fine wines and tradi-

**The White Hart**

tional ales. Manager Sara Cornwall and her husband Basil are keen to build on the restaurant's growing reputation as a friendly, comfortable establishment with an emphasis on traditional comforts and a warm and welcoming ambience. *The White Hart, High Street, Henfield, West Sussex BN5 9HP Tel/Fax: 01273 492006.*

The impressive headquarters of the **Sussex Wildlife Trust** are situated a mile to the south of Henfield at Woods Mill. Set within a 15 acre nature reserve, this three storey 18th century water mill contains a fascinating exhibition on the natural history of the locality.

Visitors to Henfield can tell that **Lyndhurst** bed and breakfast is special from first sight: a marvellous Victorian house with a multitude of expansive windows affording lots and lots of light. The decorative brickwork adds to the fairy-tale feel, and the highly unusual, ornate front porch is another fascinating feature - made from cast iron from a local ironworks in Lewes, now long defunct; very few were made in this style. Set back from the road by a picket fence and lush greenery, this charming B&B is located in the delightful village of Henfield, near Brighton. The accommodations in this roomy house - double room, family room, single room - are pleasant and simple; furnished with lovely Victorian style features and

*Lyndhurst*

linens, including antique beds and patchwork quilts. Owner Linda Slingsby has impeccable taste, which favours a plain and simple style. The kitchen and dining room are decorated in farmhouse style, and are large and welcoming - just the place for a good chat over breakfast. Evening meals by prior arrangement. The secluded gardens are a haven of peace and tranquillity. *Lyndhurst, 38 Broomfield Road, Henfield, West Sussex BN5 9UA Tel: 01273 494054.*

In the charming parish of Woodmancote, just to the east of Henfield off the A281, **Eaton Thorne House** is a delightful 15th century cottage beautifully decorated with traditional furniture. This handsome home offering bed and breakfast accommodation has low-beamed ceilings, a warm and cosy atmosphere and plenty of character. Set in peaceful and picturesque countryside not far from Gatwick airport, it plays host to travellers from all over the world. A glance through the guests' comments book reveals a veritable United Na-

**Eaton Thorne House**

tions of satisfied visitors. There is plenty of adjacent land for long walks and bird-watching, as well as three horses kept in the stables for riding. The excellent garden comprises a fine lawn and sumptuous flower beds. John and Nan Langhorne are the genial hosts, and they take great pride in keeping the large guest rooms well appointed and attractively decorated, assuring their guests' every comfort. John does the cooking, and quality is his byword. Directions are essential for finding this secluded gem; ring ahead and John or Nan will be happy to help. *Eaton Thorne House, Woodmancote, Near Henfield, West Sussex BN5 9BH Tel: 01273 492591.*

## Upper Beeding
*Map 2 ref H7*

*12 miles S of Horsham off the A2037*

Upper Beeding is a sprawling village with a pleasant main street. The now demolished Benedictine priory of Sele was founded here around 1075 by William de Braose; now occupied by a private residence, its former site lies to the north of the present *parish church*, a building which in turn suffered a brutal remodelling at the hands of the Victorians. During the early 19th century, an important turnpike road passed through Upper Beeding; the old village toll cottage, one of the last in the county to remain in service, is now an exhibit at the Weald and Downland Museum at Singleton.

To the east of Upper Beeding, the narrow road running along the spring line at the foot the South Downs ridge connects a series of attractive villages. At ***Edburton*** there is a small 13th century church; at nearby ***Fulking*** a spring gushes out across the road near the ancient village pub.

## *Poynings*          *Map 2 ref I6*
*12 miles S of Horsham off the A23*

At no other place are the Downs more dramatic than above the village of Poynings; this is the location of the famous local landmark, ***Devil's Dyke***, a steep-sided dry ravine which, according to folklore, was dug by Satan in an unsuccessful attempt to flood the Christian churches of the Weald with the sea. At almost 700 feet above sea level, the 15 acre promontory above Devil's Dyke forms an easily defendable site on which the Iron Age people built a formidable hill fort. A high earthwork wall was built to defend the gently sloping southwestern approaches of the fortifications, the remains of which can still be seen today (indeed, the course of the present day road passes through the original fort entrance).

During Victorian times, the Devil's Dyke viewpoint became a popular attraction. Not only was a railway built to connect it with Brighton, but a cable car system was installed across the ravine and down to the villages at the foot of the steep Downs escarpment. Evidence of these has long since disappeared and today, Devil's Dyke is the domain of motorists, walkers and hang-gliding enthusiasts. A little further along the South Downs Way, and inaccessible by road, lie two delightful areas of National Trust-owned downland which are worth making the effort to reach, ***Fulking Escarpment*** and ***Newtimber Hill***.

## *Hassocks*          *Map 2 ref J6*
*13 miles SE of Horsham off the A273*

Here in the charming village of Hassocks, nestling at the foot of the South Downs, the picturesque ***Thatched Inn*** public house and res-

**The Thatched Inn**

taurant has, as its name suggests, a lovely roof fashioned from Norfolk reeds. This impressive and atmospheric establishment, located down a quiet country lane (on the B2112 near Keymer) boasts exposed oak beams, inglenook fireplace and leaded windows, and attracts both local and passing clientele, including walkers, cyclists, car tourers and special interest groups. All come to experience the relaxing, friendly atmosphere, where they can enjoy a sandwich, ploughman's or perhaps a tender steak (and, on Sunday, the lunchtime roast) along with fine ales and spirits. The extensive gardens offer spectacular views over the Sussex countryside to the Ditchling Beacon. Proprietors Edward and Ishbel Daniel open this handsome, welcoming establishment to monthly meetings of the AJS and Matchless Club and the Austin 10 club. Open 7 days a week (Monday-Saturday 11-11; Sunday midday-10.30 p.m.). *The Thatched Inn, Grand Avenue, Keymer, Hassocks, West Sussex BN6 8DH Tel: 01273 842946.*

## *Clayton* *Map 2 ref J6*
*13 miles SE of Horsham off the A273*

This unusual village has a parish church containing a series of 12th century wall murals which are thought to be by the same group of artists from the St Pancras Priory in Lewes who were responsible for those at Hardham and Coombes. Rediscovered in the 1890s, the murals depict some salutary scenes of eternal damnation from the Last Judgement.

The village stands at the northern end of the one and a quarter mile long *Clayton Tunnel*, an engineering wonder of its day which was built in 1841 and opened in 1846; it still carries the busy London to Brighton rail link. A towering Victorian folly known as *Tunnel House* stands at the tunnel's northern portal. Built to house the resident tunnel-keeper, this castellated mock-Tudor fortress is still in occupation today.

A unique pair of windmills known as *Jack and Jill* stands above the village on Clayton Hill. Jack is a black-painted tower mill which fell into disuse in the 1920s and has since been converted into an unusual private home; Jill is a smaller white-painted timber-built post mill built in 1821 and removed from its original site in Dyke Road, Brighton, by a team of oxen around 1850. Now restored, it is still capable of grinding corn and is occasionally open to visitors.

A couple of interesting country houses lie within easy reach of Clayton; *Danny*, a characteristic E-shaped manor house with an impressive great hall, lies one mile to the northwest, and *Newtimber*

**Place**, a moated flint and brick-built residence, lies on the western side of the A23 a couple of miles to the west.

## Pyecombe

*Map 2 ref J6*

*13 miles SE of Horsham off the A23*

Pyecombe is a former coaching village with a good inn and a Norman church with a tapsel gate similar to the one at Coombes. Pyecombe church is a building of classically simple beauty. Standing on the prehistoric track along the South Downs from Stonehenge, along the pilgrim route to Canterbury, the church was built in 1170. Its pulpit dates from 1636; the encaustic floor tiles are 13th century. Perhaps the church's greatest treasure is the 12th century lead font, one of only three left in Sussex. It bears the traces of the whitewash used to disguise it during the Civil War, so that the lead would not be taken to be used to make bullets. The tapsel gate, as wide as a five-bar gate, swings on a central pivot allowing people to enter and leave at the same time.

Here in Pyecombe you will find the delightful ivy-clad **Forge Tearooms**, an informal and relaxed oasis in a leafy country lane on the South Downs Way. Built in 1707, it should be part of every Downswalker's itinerary. Flagstone floors, exposed beams, and the original blacksmith's open fire, combine with dozens of Downland farming artefacts and photos to make a visit to Annie Theakston's tearooms like a step back into a byegone age. A warm welcome, deli-

**The Forge Tearooms**

cious home-made cakes and Sussex cream teas make this the perfect place to break your journey. Open weekends March to September or by appointment. *The Forge* (opposite the church), *Pyecombe, West Sussex BN45 7FQ Tel: 01273 842272.*

## Cuckfield                                            Map 2 ref J4
*9 miles SE of Horsham off the A272*

Cuckfield is a sizable village with an exceptional Elizabethan and Georgian centre. The Norman lords of Lewes, who once used to hunt deer and wild boar in the forest around Cuckfield, also founded a church on high ground; this was rebuilt in the 13th century with a shingled broach spire and Horsham 'slate' roof and became Cuckfield's parish church. It was again altered in Victorian times; today it contains some fine carved monuments and stained-glass windows.

*Seventh Heaven* in Cuckfield is a charming giftshop selling a cornucopia of esoteric items including crystals, wind chimes, brooches, earrings, scarves, books, CDs and tapes, scented products, pottery and gifts from around the world. The shop is suffused

***Seventh Heaven***

with a restful and relaxing ambience, enhanced by the fragrances in the air and the natural mood music. Owner Jill Larkin has experienced for herself the healing power of crystals, and can recommend specific crystals for individual problems (physical, emotional or spiritual). She also runs crystal workshops to promote healing energy and self-healing. Jill is happy to describe the benefits of crystals and the properties of the wide range of crystals available. Her clientele include people of all ages, from all walks of life. Jill can discuss perceived problems and recommend crystal cures. She also provides referrals to other alternative therapy practitioners at the local Healing Centre. For that truly unusual, memorable gift for a special person or occasion, Seventh Heaven is definitely worth a visit. *Seventh Heaven, Clockhouse Courtyard, High Street, Cuckfield, West Sussex RH17 5EN Tel: 01444 441542.*

Before a new turnpike road was built in 1807, Cuckfield stood on the main London to south coast coaching route. A number of fine buildings remain from this era of genteel prosperity, including the King's Head coaching inn in the High Street, the ***Talbot*** former law courts and civic centre, and Ockenden Manor, now a hotel. Cuckfield's gradual development has given rise to an unusually wide assortment of building styles and materials, including brick, local sandstone, weatherboarding and tile-hanging. Those interested in discovering more about the history of this fine old settlement should make a point of visiting **Cuckfield Museum** in Queen's Hall in the High Street.

During the Elizabethan era, the leading Cuckfield iron-master, Henry Bowyer, built **Cuckfield Park**. This substantial country house and estate was subsequently acquired by the Sergison family who, during the 1840s, refused permission for the new South Coast Railway to cross their land. As a result, the railway was forced to the east and a station built at Haywards Heath, a then remote settlement on exposed heathland which within a few years had grown sufficiently to depose Cuckfield as the area's main market town.

***Mansfields Restaurant*** occupies a lovely converted ivy-clad house which retains all its original features and rooms. Immediately as you enter you step into the tiny, well-stocked bar. The three other intimate rooms are very well appointed, with open fireplaces, crisp white tablecloths and beautiful pictures on the walls. Wine is stacked around the walls, which adds to the homely, comfortable ambience. Owners Gunther and Patricia Schlender, having worked in catering in London for 30 years, moved to Cuckfield in 1996; they run this handsome establishment with their son. Gunther, a former head chef with Robert Carrier for 17 years, creates dishes reflecting German, French and English influences, and admits to a leaning towards the East. The ever changing, excellent menu includes starters such as smoked haddock, and tartlet of stilton, walnuts and spinach; main courses include grilled seatrout, roasted mallard, ragout

**Mansfields Restaurant**

of local venison, and fresh and wild mushroom pancakes; for afters there's Austrian hazelnut and chocolate pudding, pear and almond tartlet, and praline ice cream. The selection of wines and spirits is excellent. Lunches Wednesday to Friday 12.15-2; dinners Tuesday to Saturday from 7.15. Booking recommended. *Mansfields Restaurant, 1 Broad Street, Cuckfield, West Sussex RH17 5IJ, Tel: 01444 410222 Fax: 01444 410333.*

### Ansty
*9 miles SE of Horsham off the A272*

Map 2 ref J4

Situated near the delightful parish of Ansty, two miles to the south-west of Cuckfield, the impressive Sussex Archeological Society-affiliated **Legh Manor** is open to visitors during the months of May to September.

Ideal as a quiet base for visiting Brighton, Eastbourne or other points on the East Sussex coast, **Netherby** is a welcoming and supremely comfortable bed and breakfast located in the tranquil Haywards Heath suburb of Ansty. This handsome brick home is the essence of traditional comfort inside and out. The atmosphere in this small, unpretentious B&B is cheerful and friendly: rooms are

***Netherby***

well-furnished and lovely watercolours fill the house, adding to the warm ambience of the place. There is also a pleasant garden for guests to relax in. Susan Gilbert is your convivial hostess. She is more than happy to chat to her guests on a range of subjects including classical music and local history, both of which she has a keen interest in and knowledge of. Susan and her husband put a great deal of care and effort into making every guest feel special, and are happy to suggest local restaurants and public houses that might be of interest to their guests. *Netherby, Bolney Road, Ansty, Haywards Heath, West Sussex RH1Y 5AW  Tel: 01444 455888.*

## Haywards Heath

On entering Haywards Heath from the west along the A272, you first pass through the conservation area around **Muster Green**, a pleasant open space surrounded by trees which is believed to take its name from the obligatory annual 17th century custom of *'mustering the militia'*. Close by is the 16th century Sergison Arms, perhaps the oldest building in the town, which takes its name from the landed family who once owned Cuckfield Park.

Also in Haywards Heath lies **The Dolphin** an attractive and friendly pub. The beautifully restored interior has its original oak beams and flagstone flooring; there is a Victorian fire and hearth at one end of the open-plan room, and a much larger open fire at the other. The comfortable 'carver' chairs and scrubbed oak tables, attractive decor - exposed beams and uprights, attractive brickwork, dried hops and dried flowers adorning the walls - all contribute to the comfortable, homely ambience. The meals on offer - from light snacks to hearty repasts - are excellent, and served all day, along with a range of wonderful ales, wines and other liquid refreshment. The pub's long history began in the 17th century, when it was owned

**The Dolphin**

by Charles Sergison, a naval commissioner under William III. His descendent Anne Pritchard Sergison was a friend of novelist Harrison Ainsworth, and the Dolphin came to be the model for Rookwood Hall in the novel *Rookwood*, a romance immortalising the exploits of highwayman Dick Turpin. All this and a warm and congenial ambience makes the Dolphin a very welcoming haven. *The Dolphin, Butlers Green Road, Haywards Heath, West Sussex RH16 4AH Tel: 01444 255921.*

Just a little way to the east from Hayward's Heath is *Freshfield Lock*. Freshfield Lock could hardly be called a 'hidden place' to anyone who lives in this part of England, but for those visiting Sussex it is a place that might just be missed, which would be a great shame. It's well worth making the short diversion to visit *Borde Hill Gardens*, an award-winning landscaped estate which can be found on the Balcombe road, one and a half miles north of Haywards Heath. As well as a superb collection of late-spring flowering shrubs, these tranquil gardens offer a rich variety of all-season colour, 200 acres of parkland and woods, a lake with an adjoining picnic area, a children's adventure playground, an attractive plant sales area, and some spectacular views over the surrounding Sussex Weald. Open daily, 10 a.m. to 6 p.m. Admission charge payable.

***Copyhold Hollow*** is a beautiful, secluded bed and breakfast in the picturesque hamlet of Borde Hill. This 450 year old building is traditional in every sense, from its tiled exterior to the huge inglenook fireplace, casement windows, 'nursing' stool by the hearth, exposed oak beams and traditional antique furnishings within. The three spacious bedrooms are warm and welcoming; ensuite facilities have been added tastefully so as not to detract from the wonderful traditional ambience. Located in an area of outstanding natural beauty, nestling in its own hollow - which creates a natural echo

***Copyhold Hollow***

for voices and birdsong - this impressive establishment is approached from its drive over a charming willow patterned footbridge spanning a running stream, complete with resident ducks. The box hedge is reputed to be the oldest in Sussex. Owner Frances Druce goes to great pains to ensure guests are made welcome; evening meals are available upon request. Copyhold Hollow is difficult to find - and wonderful because of it. Listen carefully to the instructions Frances will provide on how to get there. A phone call will save hours of searching. *Copyhold Hollow, Copyhold Lane, Borde Hill, West Sussex RH16 1XU  Tel: 01444 413265.*

## *Lindfield*   *Map 3 ref K4*

*1 mile NE of Haywards Heath off the B2028*

Despite lying only a mile or so to the northeast of central Haywards Heath, the ancient village of Lindfield could not be more dissimilar in character. Like Cuckfield three miles to the west, Lindfield resisted the onslaught of the railway, instead preferring to retain its rural gentility. Today this picturesque village rises from a well manicured common, complete with village pond and cricket pitch, along a High Street notable for its listed Georgian redbrick and older timber-framed buildings, to an impressive 14th century parish church, complete with shingled broach spire. Indeed, there are a great many noteworthy buildings in Lindfield, particularly around the church and along the High Street.

The church house adjacent to the parish church is a former inn which still retains its original name, The Tiger.

## *Ardingly*   *Map 3 ref K3*

*3 miles NE of Haywards Heath off the B2028*

The imposing redbrick edifice of **Ardingly College** (pronounced Arding-lye), the famous public school which, like Lancing College, was founded by the pioneering churchman Nathaniel Woodard, is roughly a mile and a half from the parish church in Ardingly village, which contains some fine monumental brasses of the Wakehurst and Culpeper families, the former owners of nearby Wakehurst Place. To the west of the village, a tributary of the River Ouse has been dammed to form **Ardingly Reservoir**, a 200 acre lake which offers some good fishing. On a permanent site to the northwest, the three day South of England Show takes place each year in early June. As well as being the venue for the region's premier agricultural event, the showground hosts a range of other attractions, including showjumping competitions and antiques' fairs.

Situated beside the B2028 a mile and a half north of Ardingly, the National Trust-owned **Wakehurst Place** is sometimes referred to as 'Kew in the Country'. This beautiful Elizabethan country mansion and estate was originally built for Sir Edward Culpeper in 1590 and is now managed by the Royal Botanic Gardens, Kew. The grounds contain an unrivalled collection of rare trees, flowering shrubs and plants which are laid out in a variety of imaginative settings; there is a rich diversity of formal gardens, natural woodland, wetland, fields and meadows. A picturesque water course links a series of ponds and lakes along a nature trail providing an important conservation resource for the plants and animals of the Sussex

Weald. Open daily, 10am to 7pm (or dusk if earlier), all year round; admission charge payable (free to National Trust members).

### *Horsted Keynes*                     *Map 3 ref K4*
*2 miles NE of Haywards Heath off the B2028*

Here in the handsome village of Horsted Keynes, **The Croft** is a cosy bed and breakfast. The village boasts a Norman church and a Native American museum, as well as two delightful country pubs within walking distance of the B&B. The unusual double-gabled brickwork exterior conjures up images of hearth and home comforts, and this is precisely what visitors will find. Fidelma Ollif, originally from County Waterford, is the engaging owner. She takes great pride in catering for her guests' every comfort. Newly decorated, the interior is restful and supremely comfortable. There is a spa-

**The Croft**

cious garden for relaxing, and lovely country walks from the doorstep. Horsted Keynes is convenient for Gatwick Airport, Ardingly Showground, the Ashdown Forest and many National Trust properties. In addition, it is very close to the Bluebell steam railway line - many of the engines in the Reverend Awdry's Thomas the Tank Engine stories were based on Bluebell engines, some now over 100 years old. Commended by the English Tourist Board, this fine B&B makes an ideal base for these and other Sussex sights and pursuits. *The Croft, Lewes Road, Horsted Keynes, West Sussex RH17 7DP Tel: 01825 790546.*

## *West Hoathly*

*Map 3 ref K3*

*5 miles N of Haywards Heath off the B2028*

West Hoathly (sometimes pronounced Hoath-lye, sometimes Hoath-lee) stands at an ancient road junction almost 600 feet up on a ridge of the High Weald. This historic settlement has some panoramic views of the South Downs. It also contains some outstanding old buildings: the Norman church was founded around 1090 and re-built in the 13th century, the Cat Inn was the haunt of smugglers in the 18th century, and the stone-built *Gravetye Manor* was con-structed around 1627 for a local iron-master and is now a first-class country house hotel.

Perhaps most exceptional, however, is the *Priest House*, a de-lightful early 15th century Wealden hall-house, timber-framed and with a hefty Horsham 'slate' roof, set in a classic English country garden. The house was originally built with a large open hall, but was altered to its present layout in Elizabethan times; inside, there is a fine collection of 18th and 19th century furniture and a charm-ing museum of village life. The building is owned by the Sussex Archeological Society and is open to the public. Admission charge.

*The White Hart* is a handsome Tudor-style public house and restaurant with an impressive and distinguished past. Located in the historic settlement of West Hoathly, long renowned for its out-standing ancient buildings, this handsome establishment dates back in parts over 600 years. The restaurant occupies a 14th century former barn, its magnificent arched roof and exposed timbers hav-ing survived intact since the reign of Edward III. The other con-verted farmhouse buildings that make up this attractive establish-

*The White Hart*

ment date from the 16th century. The ceilings are low, with exposed beams, and the wood-burning inglenook fireplace takes centre stage in the pub, its evocative aromas wafting throughout this cosy and supremely comfortable establishment. Rob Jarvis and Graham Martin, the amiable and welcoming owners, have carefully refurbished and restored this characterful pub. As a Free House, The White Hart offers real ales including Harvey's of Lewes bitter ale and other Sussex-brewed beers. All the food is fresh, home-prepared and home-cooked; the menu is a gastronome's delight. *The White Hart, Ardingly Road, West Hoathly, West Sussex RH19 4RA Tel: 01342 715217.*

### Worth                                               *Map 2 ref J2*
*7 miles N of Haywards Heath off the B2036*

For those with a particular interest in historic churches, the ancient settlement of Worth merits a visit. It contains one of the most complete Saxon churches in the country which, despite having been 'restored' and having had a reproduction spire added during Victorian times, retains its original Saxon walls, windows and arches, the largest of which is 22 feet high. ***St Nicholas' Church*** was built between 950 and 1050, but for some reason isn't mentioned in the Domesday Book. It's still in use today and is open daily during daylight hours. The name Worth comes from a Saxon term meaning 'enclosure in the forest'; the village was once an important centre of the iron-smelting industry, and ***Rowfant House*** on the eastern edge of the village was built for a successful local iron-master during the late-Elizabethan era.

Three miles east, just south of the B2110 near Turner's Hill, is the exceptional National Trust-owned house and garden, ***Standen***. This remarkable late Victorian country mansion and showpiece of the Arts and Crafts movement was built by architect Philip Webb using a variety of traditional local building materials, including brick, stone, weatherboarding and facing tiles. It was completed in 1894 for a prosperous London solicitor, who used it as a family retreat before retiring here some years later. Webb was a colleague of William Morris, the famous founder of the English Arts and Crafts Movement; Morris designed the house's carpets, wallpaper and textiles. The interior has now been completely restored and, as well as the Morris furnishings, visitors can see the original electric fittings, billiard room and conservatory, all designed in the same lively style which was to become fashionable during the 1920s. The house is set within a beautiful hillside garden and enjoys spectacular views over Ashdown Forest and the valley of the upper Medway river.

## East Grinstead

*Map 3 ref K2*

*10 miles NE of Haywards Heath off the B2110*

One and a half miles north of Standen lies the old Sussex market town of East Grinstead. Despite its suburban sounding name, East Grinstead has a surprisingly long and rich history. The town was granted its market charter in 1221; throughout the late Middle Ages it was one of the most important mercantile and iron-founding centres in the High Weald. The surrounding forest and sandstone ridge provided some excellent building materials - a surprising number of sizable domestic structures from this period survive to this day. Some of the finest can be seen in a group on the southern side of the High Street; these timber-framed buildings are characteristic of the Sussex 'hall' houses which were popular in the 15th and 16th centuries, and include ***Amherst House***, ***Sackville House*** and the imposing ***Cromwell House*** which was built in 1599 with distinctive oriel windows, brick chimneys and overhanging timbering.

Opposite stands ***Sackville College***, a development of Jacobean almshouses built around a courtyard in 1609; this attractive quadrangle, with its sandstone walls, Horsham 'slate' roofs and redbrick chimneys, was constructed for retired workers from the Sackville estates at Buckhurst and Knole. The college was renovated in the 19th century and continues to house a number of local elderly people; visitors are, however, permitted to view the public rooms, including the old banqueting hall with its magnificent hammerbeam roof.

The Georgian parish church of St Swithin was constructed by James Wyatt in 1789 after the tower of its predecessor had collapsed twice, on the second occasion taking with it the majority of the building. The replacement structure is a striking example of early Gothic Revival; it has a spacious interior and a unusually tall tower which is believed to have been built at the request (and expense) of Charles Abbot, the then Speaker of the House of Commons, so that it could be seen from his nearby country estate.

***Dunnings Mill*** in East Grinstead, as its name suggests, began life as a water mill - the wheel is still in place - and has evolved from a small cottage to the large public house and restaurant it is today. Tenants Rikky Horn and Leslie Hercho are the amiable, outgoing hosts. Leslie is the chef, while Rikky looks after front of house. As a free house, this excellent pub offers a distinguished range of beers and spirits, including several popular brands of real ale. The building dates back to the 16th century - as the exposed beams and low ceilings attest. There is a large dining room seating up to 100 guests,

**Dunnings Mill**

and an extensive and ever-changing menu of hearty staples and more adventurous and creative dishes. There is another bar in the cellar for the younger set, which in no way intrudes on the other sections of the pub, which remain quiet and private. Situated just a few minutes from the centre of East Grinstead and set back from the road, the quiet, cosy Dunnings Mill is well worth a visit. *Dunnings Mill, Dunnings Road, East Grinstead, West Sussex RH19 4AT Tel: 01342 362341.*

Before the 1832 Reform Act, only the occupants of East Grinstead's 48 original burgage plots (long narrow housing allotments) were eligible to vote, making this a notorious rotten borough. As was common practice elsewhere where voting rights were dependent on the ownership of small plots of land, the local landed family, in this case the Sackvilles, would ensure they acquired enough of them to guarantee a comfortable majority. Following a century or so of gradual decline, the coming of the railway in 1855 led to a revival and today, East Grinstead is a flourishing country town with good shopping facilities and some excellent amenities for sport and recreation. There is also an interesting **Museum of Local History** in East Court, College Lane.

# Around Crawley

The new town of Crawley is home to the **Crawley Museum Centre** on Old Horsham Road, an interesting and informative repository of local artefacts and lifestyle.

**The Hillside Inn** is also well worth a visit. This handsome establishment began life as an 18th-century coaching inn serving the main London-to-Brighton road (and still takes part in the yearly London-to-Brighton rally, as a stop along the route offering refreshment to all participants and spectators), before being carefully converted and restored into the handsome and welcoming establishment that

*The Hillside Inn*

greets visitors today, and caters for a wide variety of customers as a result of its location close to Gatwick Airport. Despite its close proximity to the airport, the area surrounding the pub is predominantly parkland; the pub hosts countryside walks throughout the year. The interior is warm and welcoming, with 3 log fires, soft lighting, tasteful decor and cosy, comfortable seating. This traditional, old-fashioned and quality establishment serves superior food and drink, and the landlord with his amiable and helpful staff make sure that all their customers receive the best in service and hospitality. *The Hillside Inn, Balcombe Road, Pound Hill, Crawley, West Sussex Tel: 01293 880911.*

## Gatwick Airport                    *Map 2 ref I2*
*2 miles N of Crawley on the A23*

It was only in the early 1930's that Gatwick's obtained its first aerodrome licence. In September 1933, Morris Jackaman purchased Gatwick for £13,500 and subsequently formed Airports Ltd, which developed the aerodrome into an airport. The Air Ministry issued

Gatwick with it's first public licence on March 13th permitting the airport to be used by commercial aircraft. On Sunday May 17th 1936 passengers boarded the DH86 Express from Gatwick to Paris. The fare for the British Airways flight was £4 5 shillings (£4.25p) which included first class travel from Victoria to Gatwick by train. The official opening of the airport took place on June 6th 1936 when the Secretary of State for Air opened the world's first circular air terminal, which was immediately christened the 'Beehive' due to it's unusual shape.

After Germany's invasion of Poland in September 1939 Gatwick like all civil airports was placed under military control. Gatwick saw many different uses during the war years , culminating in a role as one of the bases for D-Day operations.

The airport was returned to civil use in 1946 and by July 1952 the Government had approved proposals to develop Gatwick as an alternate airport for Heathrow. The new Gatwick airport opened in 1958 and was the first airport in the world to combine air, main line railway and trunk road under one roof. The airport was first used on May 30th 1958 by a Transair Viscount.

Amongst other Gatwick Airports 'firsts' was the pier leading from the terminal to the aircraft stands, giving passengers direct access to the aircraft, which was the first in Britain. Gatwick was only the second airport in the world to have a full instrument landing system in two directions.

As Gatwick entered the 70's the runway was extended to accommodate the increase in intercontinental jets using the airport and this expansion has continued up to the present day with the steady growth in passenger numbers. In 1988 the North Terminal opened, which was part of a phased development planned to increase the airports capacity to 30 million by the year 2000.

The history of the ***Flight Tavern*** has many parallels with that of its near neighbour, Gatwick Airport. Originally known as Mayfield Farmhouse when Gatwick was just being established in the 1930s, it was purchased in 1962 by Captain Victor Townsend, a retired Gatwick pilot and head of Townsend Aviation, who turned it into a private club. In 1986 the tavern as it now stands came into being, perfectly placed to serve travellers from near and far afield, with excellent food, hand-pulled cask-conditioned ales and a variety of good wines, all to be enjoyed in the pleasant and comfortable surroundings. The impressive brick-and-tiled exterior of this large establishment offers a foretaste of what's inside; the handsome, tasteful decor, soft lighting and comfortable furnishings enhance the cosy

**The Flight Tavern**

atmosphere, as do the friendly, attentive staff. Visitors will find no pool tables or games machines here, but instead a good old-fashioned quality establishment with a warm and welcoming atmosphere - just the place to relax and enjoy well-earned refreshment, no matter how far you've travelled. *Flight Tavern, Charlwood Road, Lowfield Heath, Crawley, West Sussex RH11 0QA  Tel: 01293 653950*

## Ifield                                    *Map 2 ref I2*
*1 mile W of Crawley off the A23*

Just to the west lies the **Ifield Watermill** on Hyde Drive, a working waterwheel and hammer pond, featuring fascinating displays of milling machinery and local history.

Here, just a stone's throw from Crawley new town and within easy striking distance of Gatwick Airport, is **The Gate**, a restful pub on a quiet road in a country setting. Ivy-covered dormers face the entrance with its ample parking space and owner Sarah Bloomfield ensures that the welcome inside lives up to the expectations outside. There is a good selection of ales and lagers, not to mention the extensive wine list that ties in with the food that is served. The Gate has its share of loyal locals setting the world to rights, and its location also means that it gets the odd nervous air traveller taking a bit of fortification before a flight. Sarah's menu is imaginative and tempting, offering hearty favourites such as steaks and fresh fish as well as imaginative choices such as deep fried

**The Gate**

breaded goat's cheese. Food and drink can be taken outside to the attractive garden. *The Gate, Rusper Road, Ifield, Crawley, West Sussex RH11 0LQ Tel: 01293 871271.*

# CHAPTER FOUR
## Brighton & The East Sussex Downs

*Elizabeth Glynde Place*

# Chapter 4 - Area Covered

*For precise location of places please refer to the colour maps found at the rear of the book.*

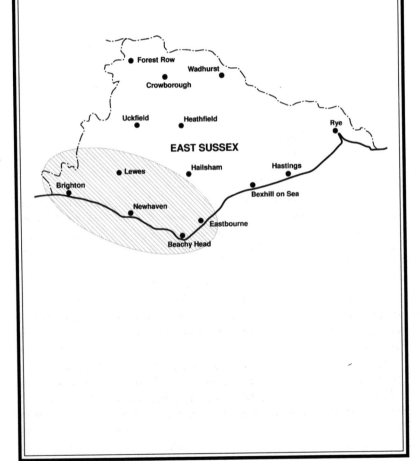

# 4
# Brighton & The East Sussex Downs

## Introduction

East Sussex is fast regaining its rightful place as Britain's most popular seacoast strip. This area of the county's Channel shoreline features three large and thriving towns: Brighton, Hove and Eastbourne. These coastal cities feature lively cultural scenes as well - every May, for instance, Brighton offers England's biggest arts festival. Demographics indicate the East Sussex coastal population is getting younger every year.

Around 70 per cent of the population of East Sussex live on the coast, but there's much more to this part of Sussex. The rural inland is home to the continuation of the South Downs Way and a wealth of charming, traditional villages and towns and hamlets rich in scenery and historical interest.

Ditchling Beacon is the region's highest point, affording marvellous views northwards across the Weald to the North Downs. Glyndebourne is a cultural centre par excellence, set near the stately beauty that is Glynde Place. Other stately homes of note include Firle Place.

The county town of Lewes is a treasure-trove of history and bucolic splendour, while back on the coast, the quieter seaside towns of Newhaven and Seaford offer relaxing days out and the dramatic Seven Sisters Country Park. The spectacular South Downs Way passes right through Plumpton, home to the internationally renowned racecourse. All this and the Long Man of Wilmington mean that the Eastern South Downs of Sussex offers a variety of landscapes and recreational options.

# Brighton

Before Dr Richard Russell of Lewes published his famous dissertation on *"The Use Of Sea Water In Diseases Of The Glands"* in 1753, Brighton was a small and unassuming fishing village which went under the name of Brighthelmstone. At that time, the sea front was constantly under threat from the encroachment of the sea, and those not directly involved in fishing settled on higher ground in the area of densely packed streets and alleyways now known as **The Lanes**. Although most of the buildings here were renewed in the early 19th century, this highly picturesque quarter between West, North and East Streets retains its maze like mediaeval street plan. The present day Lanes are inhabited by an interesting assortment of antique shops, street cafes and specialist retailers which together form a fascinating attraction.

Dr Russell's ideas gradually gained favour amongst the rich and influential until in 1783, the fashionable status of the town was

**The Royal Pavilion**

affirmed when the Prince of Wales chose to sample the beneficial effects of the new resort for himself. The young prince, who was later to become Prince Regent and then George IV, was so taken with the place that he decided to build a permanent **Royal Pavilion** in the resort. Initially a small farmhouse, it was enlarged and added to over the years. In 1787, architect Henry Holland designed a classical style building with a dome and rotunda; in 1815, John Nash, the architect responsible for London's Regent's Park and the Mall, was asked to carry out a major renovation.

Nash came up with a radical and exotic scheme based on an Indian maharajah's palace complete with minarets, onion shaped domes and pinnacles (not to everyone's liking, the upper part of the new building was once unkindly described as 'a large Norfolk turnip with four onions'). Inside, the flavour of the building moves from the Indian subcontinent to the Far East in what must be one of the finest examples of Regency chinoiserie in the world. This highly individual style reaches its zenith in the banqueting hall whose towering domed ceiling contains an elaborate chandelier from which a silver dragon can be seen hanging by its claws. The Great Kitchen with its huge array of special cooking utensils is another part of this extraordinary building which should not be missed.

The nearby **Dome** was once an arena for exercising the royal horses and is now a major concert venue; the Prince Regent's former tennis courts were converted into Brighton's acclaimed **Museum and Art Gallery**. Among its marvellous displays are art-nouveau and art-deco furniture and decorative art, musical instruments, fashion and costume, 18th and 19th century porcelain and pottery, and paintings by both English and European masters.

The town contains a number of other splendid Regency developments, most of which are dotted along the seafront on either side of the old mediaeval centre. Among the better known are Bedford Square, Regency Square, Russell Square, Kemp Town and, perhaps most famous of all, **Royal Crescent**; this elegant row of terraced houses is faced with dark 'mathematical' tiles, small hanging tiles designed to resemble fine brickwork and a characteristic architectural feature of this part of East Sussex.

Brighton also has a couple of noteworthy churches: St Nicholas' in Dyke Road is Brighton's oldest, a rare survivor from the 14th century with some interesting monuments and a superb carved Norman font. St Peter's, a short distance to the north of the Royal Pavilion, was designed in lavish neo-Gothic style in the 1820s by Charles Barry, later one of the architectus of the Houses of Parliament. At 135 feet, the walls of **St Bartholomew's Church** near the railway station are the tallest of any parish church in England. Never completed, it was built in the 19th century to the same dimensions as Noah's Ark. The building is visible from the London train and is rumoured to have been designed in this manner to remind potentially wayward trippers of the omnipresence of the Lord.

A hidden place which may be of interest to those keen on antique toys and model railways is situated in the arches underneath Brighton station. The **Sussex Toy and Model Museum** includes collections of trains, aircraft, cars, soldiers, forts, teddy bears and dolls.

Modern Brighton is a vibrant seaside town which offers visitors an enormous range of recreational activities. Apart from its long shingle beach, there are two splendid Victorian piers (one of which is no longer open to the public), a combined aquarium and dolphinarium which was founded in 1872, a popular race course, an electric railway which was the first of its kind in the country, and an impressive marina which, at 126 acres, is the largest such development in Europe.

One of Brighton's lesser known attractions is **Preston Manor**, a 13th century manor house which is set within beautiful landscaped grounds on the northern approaches to the town. The house was rebuilt in the 1730s and was left to the people of Brighton in 1932 on condition that it would remain an 'English country home'. The interior contains a permanent display of 18th century furnishings, silverware and porcelain, and the grounds have been preserved in period style and contain some fine water-lily ponds and a famous scented rose garden. One disctinctive room is decorated with squares of leather brought to England by Catherine of Aragon, first wife of Henry VIII. There are lily ponds, a walled garden, a croquet lawn and a pets' graveyard in the grounds.

Two more of Brighton's attractions are **The Booth Museum of Natural History** and **The Sea Life Centre**. The former is home to one of the finest collections of birds in Britain. Over 500, mainly assembled from 1865 to 1890, can be seen in settings that recreate their natural habitats. Other galleries include displays of butterflies, fossils, and an extensive display on nature conservation. The underground Sea Life Centre offers a fascinating exploration of life under the sea. Collections of marine life, both tropical and native, touch pools and the thrill of stingrays, sharks and giant eels at close quarters are among the marvellous exhibits.

Brighton is also graced with several lovely parks, including **Preston Park** near Preston Manor, and stately **Queen's Park**. Visitors entering the town along the nearby London Road pass a sandstone pillar with the charming inscription:

> '*Hail guest, we know not what thou art,*
> *If friend, we greet you hand and heart,*
> *If stranger such no longer be,*
> *If foe... our love shall conquer thee.*'

## Around Brighton

### Hove
*Map 2 ref J8*
*1 mile W of Brighton off the A259*

Genteel Hove is famous for its Regency squares - Brunswick and Palmeira to name but two - broad tree-lined avenues and sweeping lawns. Formerly a peaceful fishing village, major development occurred in the early 19th century when the seafront was built with its distinctive terraces painted in the colour known as Hove Regency Cream.

**Hove Museum and Art Gallery**, located in a grand villa, features English paintings, pottery, glass, coins, medals, Victorian toys and an exhibition on the history of Hove. Outside, the Jaipur Gate is a large wooden pavilion transported from Rajashtan to London in 1886; it came to Hove in 1926. The **British Engineerium** is a museum containing exhibits of models, printing presses, hand tools and full size working steam traction engines, all housed in a former pumping station. As well as architectural treats, Hove is home to the lovely **Hove Park** and **St Ann's Well's Gardens**.

A unique view of the Downs can be seen through a camera obscura at the **Foredown Tower Countryside Centre** on the outskirts of Hove.

### Rottingdean
*Map 3 ref K8*
*3 miles E of Brighton off the A259*

Built in a gap in the cliffs eastward along the coast from Brighton, Rottingdean is home to the **Grange Museum and Art Gallery**, housed in the former vicarage to St Margaret's Church. In 1919 Sir Edwin Lutyens remodelled the building and the surrounding gardens, to great effect. Rottingdean is also favoured with several handsome 18th century homes, and the 16th century Ye Black Horse Inn. Several famed artists have made their homes here over the years, including William Morris, Sir Edward Burne-Jones and Rudyard Kipling. Kipling lived for five years in *'The Elms'* overlooking the village green - the walled gardens of the house are open to the public.

## Westmeston
*Map 3 ref K6*
*5 miles NW of Brighton off the B2116*

St Martin's Church in Westmeston has an unusual shingled bell turret and a series of early murals which have been attributed to the celebrated team of artists from St Pancras Priory in Lewes. The village also boasts two fine country houses: the part 15th century Westmeston Place and the early 19th century Middleton Manor, now an arts and crafts training centre for young people with learning difficulties.

*Old Middleton* is an exceedingly grand and stately home set in lush countryside at the foot of the picturesque South Downs. This superior bed and breakfast hotel has a rich and varied history: parts of the handsome building date back to the late 16th century, as witnessed by the Elizabethan exposed beam ceilings and wall joists,

*Old Middleton*

while most of the interior dates back to 1720 - the decor is fittingly Georgian; the furnishings , too, are largely in keeping with this period. The three guest bedrooms are decorated to the highest standard: the solicitous owners Stephanie and Alastair Mckenzie-Hill have taken every care in choosing pieces of taste and quality, and in assuring their guests have a peaceful and relaxing stay. The quilted bedsteads and traditional furnishings speak of genteel comforts and convenience; the lovely pictures and objets d'arts that adorn every room are a delight. Breakfast is taken in the charming dining room, a country style refectory where guests can enjoy the hearty home-cooked meals on offer. *Old Middleton, Westmeston, East Sussex BN6 8RL Tel: 01273 843789*

## Ditchling

*Map 3 ref K6*

*6 miles N of Brighton off the B2116*

The lands around the historic village of Ditchling were once part of a royal estate belonging to King Alfred, who is also believed to have owned a small palace here. The parish church of St Margaret of Antioch has a shingled Sussex Cap spire and was rebuilt in Caen stone, flint and chalk in the 13th century (it was again much altered during the 1860s). Inside are rare chalk carvings and a Norman treasure chest. Opposite the church gate stands ***Wings Place***, an unusual Tudor house built of flint, timbering and brickwork which is also referred to as ***Anne of Cleves House***. This is because it is thought to have formed part of Henry VIII's divorce settlement with his fourth wife, although there is no evidence of her ever having stayed here.

***Dolly's Pantry and Old Ditchling Bakery*** is a charming, traditional establishment located in a 17th century oak-beamed building down a quiet country road in the historic town of Ditchling. These cosy tea rooms and bakery have been in the Clarke family for 10 years, and Roderick and Sue Clarke and their staff take pride in providing delicious repasts in a welcoming, friendly atmosphere. A bakery has been on the premises since the 17th century; bread and cakes are still baked fresh here every day, as well as a range of home-made light lunches, English breakfast served all day long, and a range of wonderful teas and coffees. Outside there is a picturesque and secluded tea garden facing the South Downs. This charming establishment is convenient for Wings Place, Ditchling Museum and Stoneywish Country Park, and is just the place

*Dolly's Pantry*

for a relaxing, peaceful snack and hot drink. Open 7 days a week. *Dolly's Pantry, 6 West Street, Ditchling, East Sussex BN6 8TS Tel: 01273 8427008.*

Old Ditchling is arranged around an ancient road junction; the area to the west of this contains some exceptional early buildings. **Cotterlings** dates from the Regency period and has a striking facade of redbrick window surrounds interspersed with black glazed tiles, **Pardons** has an unusual gazebo in the grounds, and **Court Farm** incorporates a village green and the foundations of an old tithe barn. The Five Mile Act of 1665 which banned Non-conformist worship within five miles of a town made Ditchling into something of a religious centre; the **Old Meeting House** in the Twitten is a handsome survivor from this period.

**South Cottage** is a handsome, traditional country cottage home offering bed and breakfast accommodation. This distinguished establishment is a haven of peace and relaxation. Popular with walkers, car tourers and cyclists for its tranquil atmosphere and proximity to the South Downs Way, its three spacious guest bedrooms are tastefully appointed and afford marvellous views over the lush garden, surrounding fields, and the South Downs. With superb walking and horse-riding locally (B&B for horse owners can be arranged) and within easy walking distance of village pubs, the South Downs Way and the historic village of Ditchling, South Cottage boasts the finest in comfort and restful surroundings. Mrs Stock, the warm and welcoming proprietor, makes every effort to ensure her guests have a relaxing and comfortable stay. Here in this quiet country village, sur-

**South Cottage**

rounded by hills and greenery, this excellent establishment is truly a home from home. *South Cottage, The Drove, Ditchling, East Sussex BN6 8TR Tel: 01273 846636.*

During the 1920s, Ditchling became home to a lively group of artists, printers and Bohemians whose number included Eric Gill, Sir Frank Brangwyn and Edward Johnston. The village is still inhabited by a thriving population of artists and craftspeople whose work can be seen in Ditchling's many studios, galleries and antique shops.

Visitors wanting to discover more about the locality's long and interesting history should make a point of calling in at the superb **Ditchling Museum**, located in the Victorian former village school. The museum features displays on Sussex history, rural life, period costumes and domestic interiors - including the Cottage Parlour, a painstaking reproduction of a Victorian sitting room - and a changing programme of special exhibitions and events. Ditchling has a strong tradition of arts and crafts; the Hilary Bourne gallery features the work of famous Ditchling artists, including sculptor and

**Ditchling Museum**

typographer Eric Gill, calligrapher Edward Johnston, painters Sir Frank Brangwyn and David Jones, weaver Ethel Mairet and silversmith Dunstan Pruden. The former schoolmaster's garden is planted with Victorian plants and herb beds; the attractive cafe serves tea, coffee and home-made cakes. The museum shop sells books on craftsmen, local history and also hand-made ceramics and textiles created by local artists. *Ditchling Museum, Church Lane, Ditchling, East Sussex BN6 8TB Tel/Fax: 01273 844744.*

Set in restored farm buildings, ***The Turner Dumbrell Workshops*** are home to a number of different artisans and craftworkers. Jill Pryke creates a wide variety of pots for the home, all thrown on the wheel and all intended for regular use. Her range includes vases, mugs, dishes, jugs and bowls, as well as more unusual pierced ware. Jill's work is characterised by soft-coloured glazes in blues, greens

***The Turner Dumbrell Workshops***

and greys, with delicate hand-drawn decorations inspired by the surrounding countryside: leaves, birds, trees and grasses. This method of decoration allows her to make calligraphic inscriptions too, so commemorative bowls and plates made to commission form a substantial part of her output.

Ditchling's famous silversmith Anton Pruden is a true descendant of the great British Arts and Crafts tradition. He and partner Rebecca Smith produce a striking array of modern silverwork and jewellery, both in their one off commissions and stock items. Customers for their commission work range from the Archbishop of Canterbury to the Reform Club in London. Their domestic work is sold by Harrods and the Savoy Hotel shop, to name but two. Heavy gauge materials are always used, and all items bear UK hallmarks. Traditional and modern methods are employed to make items of practicality as well as beauty. Hammer marks (known as planishing marks) are usually left in, where appropriate, in the Arts and Crafts style.

Angelo Giovino produces hand-made modern furniture using traditional techniques, combining carefully chosen hard woods with his Italian flair for design. His adjoining showroom hosts a selection of items reflecting the unique quality of Angelo's work. Commissions are welcome, from mirrors to dining room suites. On the same premises, Angelo's wife Amanda offers a complete and professional picture framing service.

Gemma Quinton and her team of dedicated craftworkers specialise in the design and creation of exclusive wedding gowns, evening gowns and classic daywear. Attention to choice of colour and theme are a priority; all the designs are exclusive and make use of beautiful fabrics. *The Turner Dumbrell Workshops, North End, Ditchling, East Sussex BN6 8TD Tel: 01273 846338/846614 Fax: 01273 846684 Website: http//www.silversmiths.co.uk*

To the north of the village, **Ditchling Common Country Park** is a 188 acre nature reserve and beauty spot, with a lake, stream and nature trail. Nearby, the long-distance Sussex Border Path follows roughly the border between West and East Sussex.

To the south of Ditchling, the land rises sharply onto the 813 foot summit of **Ditchling Beacon**, the third highest point in the South Downs. Once the site of Neolithic hill fort and later, an Admiralty fire beacon, on a clear day this long established vantage point offers a 30 mile view northwards across the Weald to the North Downs. Following the Second World War, the site was donated to the National Trust in memory of a young flyer who had been killed in action. A steep twisting lane extends from Ditchling's South Street to a car park on the crest of the ridge. This road then continues southwards down the shallow slope of the Downs all the way to Brighton.

## *Falmer* *Map 3 ref K7*
*3 miles NE of Brighton off the A27*

The University of Sussex in Falmer is an impressive collection of concrete and redbrick buildings occupying part of **Stanmer Park**, a sizable country estate which is now owned by Brighton Borough Council. This, the first of the new generation of universities to be founded during the 1960s and 1970s, was designed by Sir Basil Spence, architect of Coventry Cathedral. The site incorporates an excellent theatre, the Gardner Centre, offering the public a wide range of top-class drama, dance and musical productions throughout the year.

In the southern half of the village, the churchyard of St Laurence's Church is a designated conservation area for wild meadow flowers and grasses.

## *Peacehaven* *Map 3 ref L8*
*6 miles E of Brighton off the A259*

Planned and designed during the First World War, and originally to be named Anzac-on-Sea, in honour of the Australian and New Zealand troops stationed in the area at the time, Peacehaven is a lovely development on the cliffs between Brighton and Newhaven. Along the cliff-top promenade there is a 20 foot tall monument to King George V, a spot which also marks the Greenwich Meridian.

Right on the waterfront, ***Badger's Watch*** is a charming public house with real character. The open-plan interior takes advantage of the marvellous views from this clifftop location, affording wonderful views of the sea. As befits the building's age and history, the decor in this traditional pub features exposed oak beams, flagstone

***Badger's Watch***

flooring and quality furnishings. The roaring open hearths are just the place for a cosy and relaxing fireside drink; there is also a handsome garden to enjoy when the weather is fine. This amiable establishment has known undergone many varied incarnations: known in its day as Portobello House, 17th-century House and the Lifeboat Inn.

Originally a farmhouse built in 1759, after a short time it was converted to an inn by one William Balcombe Langridge, Clerk to the Justices at Lewes. It was he who raised, in 1803, funds to establish the first Newhaven Lifeboat, making it the third station designed expressly to undertake rescues after shipwrecks. Demolished in 1809 and rebuilt in 1817, the Lifeboat Inn was then used as the headquarters of the Controller of Customs. Later sold, it saw duty as a social club, cafe and then as a private residence up until the late 1960s. Today the Badger's Watch has returned to its original calling as a comfortable and welcoming public house, serving the finest ales and wines, and tasty traditional pub fare. *Badger's Watch, South Coast Road, Telscombe Cliff, Peacehaven, East Sussex BN10 7BE Tel: 01273 579031.*

# Newhaven

The busy port and fishing town of Newhaven lies at the mouth of the River Ouse, amid some of the prettiest scenery in Sussex. Prior to the 16th century, the river flowed into the sea at Seaford, two and a half miles away; however, the combined efforts of a great sea storm and a team of Elizabethan civil engineers succeeded in rerouting the river. A 'new haven' was thus created at a place formerly occupied by the small village of Meeching. Despite its recent origins, a number of Bronze Age tools and Roman artefacts have since been discovered in and around Newhaven, indicating that the site has in fact been in occupation for many thousands of years. The 12th century St Michael's church has a wonderful beamed roof and, in the churchyard, a memorial to the 105 men who lost their lives when HMS *Brazen* foundered off Newhaven in 1800.

During the 18th and 19th centuries, Newhaven underwent a period of rapid development as its importance as a cross-Channel port grew. Louis Philippe, King of the French, landed here after being forced to flee the forces of republicanism in 1848. The 'Citizen King' stayed overnight at the Bridge Hotel, the renowned early 17th century hostelry which still stands beside the harbour bridge. After further alterations to the port were completed at the turn of the century, Newhaven established a regular cross-Channel passenger and cargo service with the Normandy port of Dieppe, four hours away to the south.

***Newhaven Fort*** was built around 1860 as part of Palmerston's little used coastal defence system. Originally designed to defend the port against attack from the sea, the vast 10 acre structure was built with a network of underground passages, a parade ground and a series of massive gun installations. Now restored, the fortress incorporates a pub, picnic area and children's assault course, along with an interesting museum of military history; this contains a large collection of historic armaments and a special room devoted to the Allied raid on Dieppe in 1942.

***Garden Paradise*** at the edge of town in Avis Road includes the Planet Earth and World of Plants exhibitions. These all-weather attractions provide a fascinating insight into the natural history of the world. Visitors can see displays of replica dinosaurs, exotic plants, flowering cacti, and a 144 million year old fossil tree which weighs over two tonnes.

## *Piddinghoe*                                    *Map 3 ref L8*
*1 miles N of Newhaven off the A259*

The village of Piddinghoe contains **St John's Church**, one of three round-towered churches in Sussex. The tower is topped by a weather vane in the shape of a golden fish (despite having been referred to by Kipling as a 'dolphin', it is widely understood to be a sea trout). The narrow main street winds past an assortment of buildings, both ancient and modern, including a malthouse and an old forge; a recently restored brick kiln can also be seen near the church. Now the domain of pleasure craft, the old village quay was once a bustling port which was popular both with legitimate and (non-legitimate!) traders.

## *Southease*                                     *Map 3 ref L8*
*3 miles NW of Newhaven off the A259*

**Southease Church** is another of the three churches in Sussex with a round tower (the third is in Lewes). Although the building was originally thought to be pre-Norman, it is likely that it was rebuilt in the late 11th century on the site of a Saxon predecessor. Inside, there are some fine mediaeval wall paintings, an unusual organ built in 1790 and thought to be one of four still in existence, and, in the tower, a peal of bells dating from the 13th century.

# Lewes

Lewes is the county town of East Sussex. This historic settlement stands at the strategically important point where the River Ouse is crossed by an ancient east-west land route. Because of the area's close proximity to Normandy, William the Conqueror divided his newly acquired Sussex estates amongst some of his most trusted lieutenants. The lands around Lewes were granted to William de Warenne and his wife, Gundrada, who not only constructed the substantial double motte and bailey **Lewes Castle** on a hillside above the river, but also founded **The Priory of St Pancras** on the southern edge of the town. This once magnificent monastic house belonged to the abbey of Cluny in Burgundy and had a great church as large as Chichester Cathedral. The priory was the home of the renowned team of artists who painted the famous ecclesiastical murals at Hardham and Clayton during the 12th century. Following Henry VIII's Dissolution of the Monasteries in 1537, the building was forcibly demolished and its stone used for constructing residential dwellings in the town.

One building thought to have benefited in this way is ***Southover Grange***, in Southover Road, a substantial gabled residence which was built in 1572 and was the childhood home of the famous 17th century diarist, John Evelyn. Today, the house is perhaps best known for its wonderful walled garden whose beautiful lawns, trees and flowering plants provide a secluded haven in the heart of the town.

Although very little of the priory has survived, a substantial part of Lewes Castle still remains, including a section of the keep with two flanking towers dating from the 13th century and a fortified gateway, or Barbican, dating from the 14th century. Visitors climbing onto the battlements are rewarded with magnificent views over the surrounding town and countryside; the castle gardens also offer an attractive area for relaxing or picnicking. The Sussex Archaeological Society's ***Barbican House Museum*** has fascinating exhibits on the history of Sussex; next door, the ***Lewes Town Model*** is a scale model of the town as it looked 100 years ago. A sound and light show illustrates Lewes' 1,000 year history.

***The Old Stables Craft Centre*** in Lewes has built up a reputation for excellence and quality. In the pleasant atmosphere of these 18th century former stables, visitors can relax and watch craftspeople at work, browse for unusual crafts and gifts, or enjoy a tea or coffee and a light snack at 'Polly's Pantry'. Proprietors Karen and Craig Marsh make Tiffany-style lamps, mirrors, display cases and many other gifts using exquisite stained glass. Other artists in residence create beautiful millefiori jewellery and patchwork quilts and cush-

***The Old Stables Craft Centre***

ions. Among the range of items on sale you will find silver and pewterware, pottery, wood-turned objects, glassware, porcelain, textiles, prints and cards, as well as speciality foods, apothecary items, embroidered pictures and much more. Open Monday-Saturday 9.30-5.30; Good Friday, Easter Monday, August Bank holiday and Sundays from March through to the end of December 11-4.00. *The Old Stables Craft Centre, Market Lane, Lewes, East Sussex BN7 2NT Tel/Fax: 01273 475433.*

In 1264, Lewes was the site of a particularly bloody confrontation between the armies of Henry III and Simon de Montfort. The Battle of Lewes took place on Mount Harry, an exposed hillside on the western side of the town, and resulted in the deaths of as many as 5,000 troops (years later, the skeletons of an estimated 1,500 men were unearthed near Lewes gaol, and hundreds more were discovered by railway engineers in a field near Plumpton). Henry's defeat led to his enforced signing of the Mise of Lewes, a document which strengthened the importance of the barons and laid the foundations of modern parliamentary democracy.

Like Ditchling, Lewes has an *Anne of Cleves House*, an early 16th century Wealden 'hall' house which formed part of Henry VIII's

***Anne of Cleves House, Lewes***

divorce settlement with his fourth wife (also like Ditchling, the property was never lived in by the estranged queen). The structure has been much altered over the centuries and has evolved into an attractive concoction of buildings set around a reconstructed Tudor garden and known as The Museum of Local History, run by the Sussex Archaeological Society. Its rooms and galleries have been arranged to create an impression of domestic and working life in Lewes in the 17th and 18th centuries.

Lewes developed strong Protestant roots following the Reformation and the burning of 17 Protestant martyrs in the town during the Marian persecutions of 1555-1557 established an anti-Catholic fanaticism which can still be detected in the town's modern bonfire night festivities. In what must be the most extravagant 5th November celebrations in the country, rival bonfire societies march through the streets carrying flaming torches and specially made 'guys'.These are then carried to the edge of town and thrown onto huge bonfires - a spectacular annual custom.

There are several handsome old churches in the town, including St Michael's, with its distinctive round tower; St Anne's, at the top of St Anne's Hill, which is lined with lovely 18th century cottages; and St Thomas', founded in the 12th century.

In the 18th century Lewes became something of a centre for radical political thought. During this period, a local excise officer, Tom Paine, became renowned as a human rights campaigner and leading supporter of the American and French Revolutions. Paine lived at *Bull House* in the High Street, now a restaurant, and married the daughter of his landlord before settling in America. On his return, he wrote the revolutionary work in support of the French Revolution, *The Rights of Man* in 1792 and was forced to flee across the Channel.

At around this time, Lewes was establishing itself as a prosperous county town. A number of its finest residential buildings, including *Lewes House* and *School Hill House*, were constructed by wealthy professional people who lived and worked in the town. Many older timber-framed buildings were refaced with characteristic 'mathematical' tiles, small hanging tiles which were designed to resemble fine brickwork. The streets of old Lewes are connected by a number of narrow pedestrian alleys, or twittens, which provide a fascinating walking tour of the town (a guide published by Lewes Town Council is available at the Tourist Information Centre in Lewes House). Lewes also possesses a renowned independent brewery, Harvey's Bridge Wharf Brewery, which was founded on the banks of the Ouse in Georgian times and was rebuilt in Victorian Gothic style during the 1880s.

# Around Lewes

### *Hamsey*                                                    Map 3 ref L6
*2 miles N of Lewes off the A275*

St Peter's Church in the charming hamlet of Hamsey stands in a wonderful position overlooking the Ouse, and is approached through the neighbouring farmyard of the 400 year old Hamsey Place Farm, where visitors must also call for the keys to the church.

### *Ringmer*                                                   Map 3 ref L6
*2 miles NE of Lewes off the B2192*

Ringmer is a sizable village centred around a pleasant green which still retains a genteel charm despite having undergone considerable development in recent years. The parish church of St Mary contains a poignant memorial to the acclaimed village cricket team who joined up en masse to fight in the First World War; of the 34 club members who went to war, only 6 were to return alive.

During the 17th century, Ringmer played an important, if roundabout, part in early American history. Two young women brought up here married men who went on to become influential figures in the development of the United States: Ann Sadler married John Harvard, the founder of Harvard University, and Guglielma Springett married William Penn, the founder of Philadelphia. However, Ringmer's most famous inhabitant appears to have been Timothy, a tortoise belonging to the aunt of the 18th century naturalist, Gilbert White, which was the subject of a long and engaging study immortalised in White's *The Natural History of Selborne*. Timothy's shell is now part of the natural history collection at the British Museum.

### *Barcombe*                                                  Map 3 ref L6
*3 miles N of Lewes off the A275*

Here among the network of country lanes which connect the many small farming settlements of the fertile Ouse Valley, the village of Barcombe is a peaceful community which is locally renowned for its excellent freshwater fishing. Like many of its contemporaries in Sussex, the village church is dedicated to St Mary, has a shingled broach spire and was heavily restored by the Victorians. There are marvellous views of the Downs from the churchyard.

Just to the north Barcombe Mills, at the site of a Roman crossroads and on the River Ouse, with its pools and weirs, has been a popular picnicking place since the Edwardian era. At that time, artists would come from miles around to paint the dilapidated flour mill buildings in this splendid Ouse Valley setting. Although the old mills have now been removed, there are still some wonderful views over the surrounding landscape towards **Mount Caburn**, the chalky outcrop which can be seen rising sharply from the valley floor to the southeast.

**Wheeltappers** is an incomparable restaurant located in a marvellous converted railway station. Set in lush countryside, with great views of the South Downs, the station, built in 1856 by the London, Brighton and South Coast railway, is a stunning example of Victorian railway architecture. Renovated by owners Allan and Jenny

*Wheeltappers*

Slater, the exterior has been lovingly restored to its original colours; the timbers and brickwork are mostly original. The spaces between platforms have been filled in to create a charming garden and children's play area. 'The Country Shop' florist occupies the track opposite. The Slaters, with help from their young daughter Sarah, offer a menu that is a mixture of traditional English dishes plus exotic specials from around the world, and specialise in catering for weddings and outdoor parties. *Wheeltappers, Barcombe Mills Station, Near Lewes, East Sussex BN8 5BL Tel: 01273 400950.*

### Plumpton
*4 miles NW of Lewes off the B2116*

Map 3 ref K6

Plumpton has an elegant 16th century moated manor house, **Plumpton Place**, which was substantially remodelled in the 1920s by Sir Edwin Lutyens. The then owner, Edward Hudson, was a wealthy magazine proprietor who had previously commissioned Lutyens to renovate his other country property, Lindisfarne Castle, off the Northumberland coast. Plumpton's famous **National Hunt Racecourse** is situated a mile and a half to the north on Plumpton Green; spectators arriving by train should look out for the Victorian signal box which has been designated a listed building following the persistent efforts of local railway enthusiasts. In Plumpton's Half Moon pub, an enormous painting of over 100 of the pub's regular customers, done in 1977, is displayed on the wall.

### Streat
*5 miles NW of Lewes off the B2116*

Map 3 ref K6

This tiny hamlet is mentioned in the Domesday Book, and has been inhabited since the Stone Age. Its distinctive buildings include an Early English church and the Elizabethan flint built manor house, **Streat Place**. Just south of the village is a wooded area of beech, lime and fir trees planted to celebrate Queen Victoria's Golden Jubilee in 1887.

### Wivelsfield Green
*8 miles NW of Lewes off the B2112*

Map 3 ref K5

**Park Farm** bed and breakfast in Wivelsfield Green will suit the most discerning of tastes. This truly luxurious B&B is located down a quiet country lane. The good sized rooms afford magnificent views to the South Downs. Owners Alan and Elizabeth Robinson take great pleasure in entertaining, and make every effort to ensure that their guests have a memorable and enjoyable stay. Guests are welcome to enjoy the pleasant gardens, while the lovely terrace is just the place to enjoy a quiet read and morning coffee. There is a well-appointed guests' lounge with an enormous fireplace.

This spacious country house manages to be both elegant and comfortable. The accommodations comprise one twin-bed room, one double, and one single; families (with children over 12) are welcome. Breakfasts are delicious and filling; packed lunches or hampers for nearby Glyndebourne are also available upon request. From here it's an easy run to Gatwick Airport, Haywards Heath and the many lovely Sussex villages in the area, as well as to Eastbourne, Brighton

***Park Farm***

and other points along the coast. *Park Farm, Hundred Acre Lane, Wivelsfield Green, Haywards Heath, East Sussex RH17 7RU Tel: 01273 890195 Fax: 01273 890693*

## Kingston-near-Lewes

*Map 3 ref K7*

*1 mile SW of Lewes off the A27*

Kingston-near-Lewes is a charming village situated along the western side of the River Ouse. St Pancras Church has a tapsel gate; inside there is a stained-glass window depicting a scene from the beautiful local countryside, and a Jacobean chest. Kingston Manor is a 16th century half-timbered house constructed in part with materials brought from Lewes Priory.

## Iford

*Map 3 ref L7*

*2 miles S of Lewes off the A27*

This charming settlement has a flint built Norman church, St Nicholas' and a 19th century manor house built in Tudor style which is the official residence of the Vice-Chancellor of Sussex University.

## Glynde

*Map 3 ref L7*

*4 miles E of Lewes off the A27*

The internationally renowned village of Glynde, although filled with well preserved traditional Sussex cottages, has a very untypical 18th century church, **St Mary the Virgin**, built in Palladian style. The churchyard contains the grave of one of Glynde's most noted sons, John Ellman, who was a pioneer of selective breeding and was responsible for producing the black-faced Southdown sheep, the breed on which most of the flocks in New Zealand and Australia are based.

**Glynde Place**, the imposing brick and flint mansion near the church, was built in 1579 for William Morley. The house has an elegant wood panelled long gallery and contains some exceptional works of art, and the grounds are beautifully laid out and incorporate an aviary and a pottery. Glynde Place is owned by Viscount Hampden and is open to the public on a limited number of days each year (opening times displayed on site).

The distinctive local landmark known as **Mount Caburn** lies to the west of Glynde and can be reached along a footpath from the village. Many thousands of years ago, this steep sided chalk outcrop was separated from the rest of the Downs by the action of the River Glynde. This process created an artificial looking mound almost 500 feet in height whose natural defensive properties have long been exploited by man. The earthwork defences of an Iron Age hill-fort can still be made out near the summit, and evidence of an earlier Stone Age settlement has also been detected.

The part Tudor, part Victorian country house lying one mile to the north of Glynde village is the home of the world famous **Glyndebourne Opera House**. This unique institution was founded by John and Audrey Christie in 1934, and since then it has built up an international reputation for presenting the finest opera in the most idyllic of English surroundings. Each summer season (May-August), audiences wearing evening dress arrive by train from London and leave their champagne to cool in the lake while they listen to the first half of the evening's performance; they then picnic in the grounds during the long interval before returning to the auditorium to enjoy the second half. Fans preferring their opera in a less precious atmosphere often choose to attend the autumn performances by Glyndebourne's Touring Company. The beautiful grounds of Glyndebourne are regularly open to visitors throughout the year

### Rodmell
*Map 3 ref L7*

*3 miles S of Lewes off the A27*

The influential Bloomsbury group figures Virginia and Leonard Woolf once owned a country retreat at Rodmell. The Woolfs acquired the **Monk's House**, a small early 18th century farmhouse, in 1919 and gradually converted it from a primitive cottage without running water or sanitation into a pleasant, albeit modest, village house. Throughout the following 20 years, Virginia Woolf, the author of such works as *To The Lighthouse*, *Mrs Dalloway* and *Orlando*, suf fered from increasingly serious bouts of depression and mental illness, until in 1941 she tragically committed suicide by drowning herself in the River Ouse. The gardens are lush with hollyhocks, dahlias and hydrangeas; there are also walled areas with ponds, statues and an orchard. Monk's House is now administered by tenants on behalf of the National Trust.

## Firle
*Map 3 ref M7*

*4 miles SE of Lewes off the A27*

Set in some of the most attractive countryside in East Sussex, this pretty village is a point along both the South Downs Way and the Rabbits Walk Way, which follows the line of a minor Roman road.

***Firle Beacon***, at 712 feet, is one of the highest points in the eastern South Downs. One of the Admiralty fire beacons which warned of the approaching Spanish Armada was sited on this exposed hilltop in the 16th century, and several ancient remains have also been discovered here, including a 100 foot Stone Age long barrow, a group of Bronze Age round barrows (known locally as the Lord's Burghs), and a Roman observation post. A number of Iron Age field terraces, or lynchets, can also be be made out, although modern farming methods are now placing these under threat. The summit can be reached by making a short detour from the South Downs Way or by climbing one of the steep paths from Alciston or West Firle; those making it to the top are rewarded with breathtaking views over the Downs to the English Channel.

***Gibraltar Farmhouse*** is a marvellous 17th century flint and timber-framed converted farmhouse and granary offering superb B&B or self-catering accommodation. Located in the conservation

**Gibraltar Farmhouse**

area in the unique village of Firle, this family run establishment is set in two acres of peaceful, well laid out gardens, with swimming pool, croquet and table tennis. The granary comprises two self-catering apartments: the studio - a large family room with a double and a single bed, sitting area, dining alcove with cooking facilities and private bathroom - and the cottage, with two bedrooms, large sitting room, dining area with cooking facilities and a separate bathroom. Both apartments are cosy and comfortable, with oak-beamed ceilings. In the farmhouse itself there are two lovely ensuite bedrooms available as B&B accommodation.Close to Glyndebourne, Charleston and the South Downs way, Gibraltar Farmhouse is a wonderful base for exploring the rolling Downland, cosy pubs, all the 'Bloomsbury' haunts and the sleepy, charming county town of Lewes. *Gibraltar Farmhouse, Firle, Nr Lewes, East Sussex BN8 6NB Tel: 01273 858225.*

## West Firle

*Map 3 ref M7*

*4 miles SE of Lewes off the A27*

The hamlet of West Firle has a good pub and a noteworthy part Norman church which contains several impressive monuments to the Gage family, the owners of nearby **Firle Place**. This elegant country mansion was built in the 16th century by Sir John Gage (1479-1556) who, somewhat surprisingly for a Roman Catholic, was Henry VIII's Vice-Chamberlain. Sir John rose to distinction in the reign of Henry VIII when he held high military posts in wars against the French and Scots. He became Constable of the Tower of London, where he had charge of Lady Jane Grey before her execution, and was one of the Council of Regency during the minority of Edward VI. He was again Constable under Queen Mary when Princess Elizabeth was kept under his surveillance in the Tower for two months. It was his standing at court that enabled Sir John to enlarge Firle Place. Two striking alabaster effigies of Sir John and Lady Philippa are among the finest features in the church.

The family were staunch Catholics until the eighteenth century, when they conformed to the Church of England and once more took part in public life. The first Viscount had two sons, one of whom succeeded him. The other, Thomas, became Commander in Chief of the British Forces at the outset of the American War of Independence in the 1770s. He was in command at the outbreak of the War of Independence, including the battle of Bunker Hill. Firle Place was significantly remodelled around this time and when Sir Thomas returned to this country, he brought with him a collection of early American artefacts which were used to furnish the house.

Thomas' eldest son Henry succeeded as third Viscount, and it is from him that the present family are descended. The Gages held another property; Hengrave Hall in Suffolk. It was from this branch of Gages that Sir Thomas Gage, a well known botanist, ordered various plums to be sent from France, in the 19th century. These were planted at Hengrave but due to a label being mislaid from off a green plum, the gardeners then renamed it 'Greengage'. There is still a shoot from the original 'plum' to be seen at Hengrave Hall.

You approach Firle Place by way of a long drive, which is very beautiful, in spite of its once fine elms having suffered as have so many others. The core of the house is a Tudor manor house and must have been built by Sir John Gage. The drawing for Sir John's tomb, by Gerard Johnson, in the church can be viewed hanging in the house. The exterior of the house is certainly part of Sir John's house and still has the original hammerbeam roof above the 18th century plaster ceilings. There is one remaining Tudor gable on the south aspect.

The deer park in which the house stands was designed in the 18th century in the style of famed landscape architect Lancelot 'Capability' Brown. It features a castellated tower and an ornamental lake. Firle is very much a family house, and because of that its warmth provides a wonderful setting for the collection of paintings by Europeans and British Old Masters. It is an important collection, considered to be one of the finest in south east England. There are rare and notable examples of French and English furniture and Sevres porcelain.

## Telscombe
Map 3 ref L8
*5 miles S of Lewes off the A259*

A two mile long cul-de-sac leads southwestwards from Southease to the remarkably well preserved village of Telscombe. This ancient Downland settlement owes its unspoilt nature to Ambrose Gorham, a local landowner who, in 1933, left most of the village to Brighton Borough Council in his will. The locality was formerly an important sheep-rearing and horse-training centre; the last man in England to be hanged for sheep stealing in 1819 is believed to have come from the village. Nearby Telscombe Tye was a popular exercising ground for locally trained racehorses.

## Selmeston
Map 3 ref M7
*5 miles E of Lewes off the A27*

The ancient hamlet of Selmeston (pronounced 'Simson') was the site where, during the 1930s, archaeologists discovered tools, weapons and pottery fragments in the local churchyard of 13th century **Selmeston Church**, which are thought to date from the New Stone Age. Despite having been heavily 'restored' by the Victorians, the church still retains its original octagonal carved-oak roof supports.

An unexpected treat at Selmeston is **Silletts Cottage Restaurant**, a grade II listed Sussex farmhouse, with part of the building dating back to 1602 when it was first built and named 'Church Farm' because its land was adjacent to the church. The date of the building is known, as it has been found carved on an exposed beam in the loft. The original building consisted simply of two downstairs front rooms, which are now a marvellous restaurant offering all the ingredients for a perfect meal in this lovely country setting. It is open for lunch and dinner seven days a week. Here can be had wonderful home-cooked meal with a fine bottle of wine in a quiet, charming, relaxed atmosphere, which would be as pleasurable in summer as winter. In the summer guests can feast their eyes on views of the Downs, and in the winter they can relax in front of the crackling log fire in the cocktail lounge.

***Silletts Cottage Restaurant***

Ron Sillett's chefs Neil Wakefield and Steve Anderson prepare all of the dishes. They are always looking for new recipes, so if you have one tucked away in a kitchen drawer do take it with you and show Ron. Silletts Cottage is quite small, and only accommodates a maximum of forty customers. Lunch is from a snack to a full a la carte with no minimum charge. Dinner is a fixed price with no hidden extra costs. Personal service is terribly important to Ron and his staff. They look after their guests superbly and genuinely want to know if there is anything they can do to please them further. You will enjoy every minute of any visit here, and will no doubt join the ranks of those who return again and again. *Silletts Cottage Restaurant, Church Farm, Selmeston, Nr Polegate, East Sussex BN26 6TZ Tel: 01323 811343.*

Approximately one mile west of Selmeston can be found the extraordinary country home of the Bloomsbury Group members Clive Bell, Vanessa Bell and Duncan Grant, two of whom were responsible for the murals at Berwick. **Charleston Farmhouse** (which shouldn't be confused with Charleston Manor near Westdean) is located at the end of a long driveway, the entrance to which is on the southern side of the A27. During the 1930s, the occupants transformed the interior of this unexceptional building into a work of art by utilising their skills as painters and designers. They covered almost every wall, floor and ceiling with their own murals, fabrics, carpets and wallpapers, and then completed the job with some fine original framed paintings, including a self-portrait by Vanessa Bell and one of Grace Higgens, their valued housekeeper.

They also created a delightful flint walled cottage garden around the farmhouse which they carefully laid out with mosaic pathways, tiled pools, sculptures and a scented rose garden. During the 1920s and 30s, this unique country retreat welcomed some of the most eminent artists and thinkers of the day, including the economist John Maynard Keynes and the young composer Benjamin Britten.

## *Alciston* *Map 3 ref M7*
### *4 miles SE of Lewes off the A27*

The original settlement of the 'forgotten village' of Alciston was abandoned following the Black Death; a new one was built some years later on the opposite side of the 13th century **Alciston Church**. To avoid the likelihood of flooding, this was built on the foundations of an earlier Saxon structure which stood at the top of a small hill. The remains of a substantial mediaeval dovecote can be seen nearby; during the late Middle Ages, large numbers of pigeons were kept here to provide a much prized supplement to the dreary winter diet. The fertile agricultural land around Alciston once belonged to the estates of Battle Abbey. At that time, the tenant farmers paid 'rent' to the abbot in the form of one-tenth of their annual farm output, and at harvest time each year, this was brought to Alciston and deposited in the abbey's huge mediaeval tithe barn. This magnificent structure is over 170 feet long and is one of the largest of its type in Sussex; it can be seen in a delightful farmyard setting on the southern side of the village, close to the point where the road into the hamlet narrows to a rough track. As well as being the focus of the estate, the adjacent farmhouse once served as a retirement home for the monks.

## Berwick
*Map 3 ref M8*

*5 miles SE of Lewes off the A27*

Berwick (pronounced Bur-wick) is a village whose Norman **Church of St Michael and All Angels** contains a famous series of wall paintings. Despite the church having been built in the 12th century and restored in the 1850s, the murals are firmly rooted in the 20th century. They were commissioned, somewhat controversially, by the Bishop of Chichester shortly after he came to office in 1929. The Bishop made the brave decision to engage the Bloomsbury Group painters Duncan Grant and Vanessa Bell who, with the help of Bell's children, Quentin and Angelica, finally completed their task in 1943. In keeping with a long tradition, the artists placed a number of clearly identifiable local people and places within a set of familiar biblical settings.

## Wilmington
*Map 3 ref N8*

*7 miles SE of Lewes off the A27*

The historic remains of **Wilmington Priory**, a once imposing Benedictine priory built between the 12th and 14th centuries, are rumoured to be inhabited by a number of legendary ghosts. Parts of the building, including the hall, gatehouse and courtyard, have now been restored by the Sussex Archaeological Society and the site includes an interesting museum of agricultural history.

Originally part of the Priory buildings, the Church of St Mary and St Peter has in its North Chapel an remarkable stained-glass window depicting different species of butterflies and bees. There are marvellous views from the churchyard west to Firle Beacon.

The mysterious figure of the **Long Man of Wilmington** can be seen from the Priory grounds. This remarkable 226 foot high 'geoglyph' of a man carrying a staff in each hand was carved into the chalky hillside of Windover Hill some time between pre-Roman times and 1779, the year it was first documented. Although his origins are thus uncertain, it is believed he is about 1,400 years old. Perhaps most astonishing is the fact that the design takes account of the slope of the hill, and so accurately maintains the proportions of a man even when viewed from below. To date, no one knows who was responsible for the carving or why it was done; various theories suggest that it is a figure of a pilgrim, a Saxon chieftain or even the

'Midsummer Man' of pagan folklore. In 1969, the carving was strengthened with over 700 concrete blocks. A quarter mile long footpath leads up to the site.

***Drusillas Zoo Park***, a fine small zoo renowned for its collections of exotic birds and smaller mammals, lies about a mile west of Wilmington, at Drusillas Roundabout, Alfriston. There is also a children's adventure play area, a miniature railway and an award winning family restaurant. The zoo is fully accessible for the disabled, and there is a Sensory Trail for the visually impaired.

## Around Seaford

Seaford, a once thriving coastal port - with its own Martello Tower - went into decline after the River Ouse diverted to its present course in the 16th century. Following the arrival of the railway in the mid-19th century the town experienced a gradual revival; today it is a comfortable seaside resort of Victorian and between the wars buildings which is popular with holidaymakers.

***Seaford Local History Museum*** is housed in the town's Napoleonic Martello Tower (built in 1806), right on the seafront, and features many interesting exhibits on local history.

***Malvern House*** is a lovely country cottage offering bed and breakfast accommodation. Particularly suitable for a peaceful and restful break - set in a quiet location on the outskirts of the seaside town of Seaford, close to the South Downs Way, historic Lewes and lively Brighton - this warm, welcoming, spacious and traditional Sussex style house, set in lovely gardens, has a true family home

***Malvern House***

atmosphere. The guest bedrooms in this handsome establishment are well-appointed, cosy and supremely comfortable. Secluded, yet convenient for many local places of interest, with fine local pubs and restaurants close by, Malvern House and its amiable, conscientious proprietors offer extras such as a laundry service and iron, picnic lunches on request, and a two course Sunday lunch. Nonsmoking environment. *Malvern House, Alfriston Road, Seaford, East Sussex BN25 3QG Tel: 01323 492058 Fax: 01323 492000.*

Just one mile southeast of Seaford, the cliffs rise dramatically to nearly 300 feet at **Seaford Head**, the promontory which lies at the western end of one of the most spectacular stretches of coastline in

**Seaford Head Nature Reserve**

the British Isles. Evidence of a prehistoric hilltop encampment and a Roman burial ground have been discovered on the site which now forms part of the **Seaford Head Nature Reserve**; this 303 acre reserve of salt marsh, grassland and shingle beach, an important habitat for birds, animals, insects and flowers, many of them rare, extends to the River Cuckmere and offers some of the most scenic cliff-top walking in Sussex.

### Westdean
*Map 3 ref M8*

*2 miles E of Seaford off the A259*

The village of Westdean lies at the end of a narrow cul-de-sac and is believed to have once contained a palace belonging to Alfred the Great. The village's All Saints' Church is part Norman and has a broad, rectangular tower with an unusual 'half-hipped' spire. Inside, there is a bust in bronze sculpted by Jacob Epstein. Other noteworthy buildings in the vicinity include the flint built church rectory, which dates from the 13th century, and **Charleston Manor**, half a mile to the north, which features a combination of Norman, Tudor and Georgian building styles.

## Exceat
*Map 3 ref M9*

*2 miles E of Seaford off the A259*

The small settlement of Exceat stands on the River Cuckmere at the northeastern corner of the Seaford Head Nature Reserve. Here, **The Living World** is a unique natural history centre which contains a fascinating collection of live butterflies, spiders, reptiles, stick insects and marine creatures, all of which can be viewed at close quarters and sometimes even handled. The centre is located in a group of converted farm buildings.

Exceat has had an unusually turbulent history; during the 14th century it was almost wiped out by the Black Death, then, 120 years later, a violent cross Channel raid almost achieved the same result. Between the hamlet and the sea, the River Cuckmere makes a spectacular serpentine meander through the area known as Cuckmere Haven. This striking flood plain forms the western boundary of the **Seven Sisters Country Park**, a broad tract of County Council and National Trust-owned Heritage Coastline which incorporates the famous Seven Sisters chain of white chalk cliffs. The cliffs, which are now receding at around 3 feet per year, can also be accessed from the top of the Downs at Crowlink and from the east at the popular picnicking spot of Birling Gap. The downland above the Seven Sisters is strewn with evidence of early settlement, including a number of Neolithic bowl and round barrows.

The *'Europe Garden'* in Exceat opened in 1992 to commemorate the relinquishing of trade barriers within the European Community.

## Friston
*Map 3 ref N9*

*3 miles E of Seaford off the A259*

The village of Friston has a part Norman St Mary the Virgin Church with a low capped tower. The churchyard contains the grave of the composer, Frank Bridge, and is entered through a rare tapsel gate, a gate which pivots around a central upright. The nearby pond was the first in England to be designated an ancient monument. The village also contains an impressive manor house, **Friston Place**, which was built in the mid 17th century around an existing timber-framed structure.

The 1,600 acre **Friston Forest** lies to the west of the village between Friston and Exceat. When this ancient beechwood forest was
acquired by the Forestry Commission in the 1920s, they planted a
number of quick growing conifers to protect the young broad-leaved
trees from the fierce coastal winds. Over the years, the conifers have
gradually been removed to reveal a magnificent mature beech forest which now incorporates some delightful waymarked walks and
picnic areas. The Forest Walk, just under 3 miles long, skirts the
grounds of Charleston Manor, continues along Charleston Bottom,
and ends above Westdean.

## Lullington
*Map 3 ref N8*

*4 miles E of Seaford off the A259*

This hamlet is renowned for having one of the smallest churches in
Britain. The 16 foot square structure is in fact the chancel of a much
larger mediaeval church which fell into disrepair following the Black
Death. The Victorians rescued what remained of the building and
converted it into its present form. The chalky heathland above
Lullington is a National Nature Reserve which is noted for its distinctive downland flora and fauna.

## Alfriston
*Map 3 ref M8*

*4 miles NE of Seaford off the A259*

Alfriston is one of the oldest and best preserved (and consequently,
most popular) villages in Sussex. The settlement was founded in
Saxon times and grew to become an important river port and market town. The old *market cross*, or at least the substantial part of
it which remains, stands beside a tall chestnut tree in the middle of
Waterloo Square; it is one of only two such structures to survive in
Sussex (the other, somewhat grander example is at Chichester). This
delightful market square, along with the old High Street leading off
to the south, is lined with ancient inns, shops and residential buildings which were constructed in an assortment of materials and styles
over the centuries. Perhaps the most striking is the 15th century
Star Inn, a former hostel for mendicant friars, whose ceiling timbers are decorated with wonderful carved animals.

Others include the 14th century George, the timber-framed Ship,
and the Market Cross, a popular smugglers' haunt which has no
fewer than six staircases and a room with five separate means of
escape (indeed, it is also known as Ye Olde Smugglers). In the early
19th century, this was the base of a notorious gang led by Stanton
Collins, a ruthless local villain who is said to have lured an excise
officer to his death on the cliffs above Seaford and was eventually

transported to Australia for stealing sheep. At one time, large quantities of contraband were brought upriver to Alfriston in the dead of night and unloaded onto waiting packhorses. Such atmospheric scenes inspired Rudyard Kipling, a one time resident of nearby Rottingdean, to pen his evocative poem, *A Smuggler's Song*:

> *If you wake at midnight, and hear a horse's feet,*
> *Don't go drawing back the blind, or looking in the street.*
> *Them that asks no questions, isn't told a lie,*
> *Watch the wall my darling, while the gentlemen go by!*
> *Five and twenty ponies, trotting though the dark,*
> *Brandy for the parson, baccy for the clerk,*
> *Laces for the lady, letters for a spy,*
> *Watch the wall my darling, while the gentlemen go by!*

Alfriston's former status as a market town is reflected in the scale of its 14th century parish church, an unusually spacious structure which is often referred to as 'the Cathedral of the Downs'. St Andrew's Church stands in a prominent position beside the Cuckmere River at the centre of a raised green known as the **Tye**. As recently as the 1930s, local shepherds would be buried here with a scrap of raw wool in their hand, a custom which served to inform the keeper of the gates of heaven that the deceased's poor church attendance was due to the obligations of his occupation.

The old **Clergy House** stands within an attractive herbaceous cottage garden on the southern edge of the Tye. This charming thatched and timber-framed building was constructed as a mediaeval 'hall' house in the 14th century and was the first property to be acquired by the National Trust in 1896, reputedly for a price of only £10. Thanks to Alfred Powell's skilful renovation, its crown post roof and original timbers have been saved. Today, the building houses an interesting exhibition on mediaeval construction techniques.

Other noteworthy buildings in Alfriston are its early 19th century Congregational Church and the **Alfriston Heritage Centre and Old Forge**; this interesting museum on the social history of the locality is housed in a restored 15th century blacksmith's forge and can be found next to the Dene car park, a little to the north of Waterloo Square.

## Litlington                                    *Map 3 ref M8*
*4 miles NE of Seaford off the A259*

The small village of Litlington is perhaps best known for its Victorian tea gardens. This elegant outdoor cafe was founded over 150 years ago making it the oldest such establishment in Sussex. Here, customers are offered the finest English cream teas and homemade refreshments in a relaxed old-fashioned atmosphere. Litlington's 13th century village church of **St Michael the Archangel** contains a font made from 'Sussex marble', the distinctive limestone which is found around Petworth. An outline of a white horse, the only example of its kind in the county, is carved into the chalk hillside on the western bank of the Cuckmere opposite Litlington; during the Second World War, this was covered up to prevent it being used as a navigational aid by enemy bomber pilots.

# Eastbourne

This stylish and genteel seaside resort takes its name from the stream, or *bourne*, which has its source in the old reservoir in the area of open land now known as Motcombe Gardens. The town developed relatively recently as a seaside resort. Prior to 1780, when the children of George III spent the summer here, Eastbourne consisted of two separate villages, the larger of which lay over a mile inland. A period of gradual development then followed, which gained momentum after the town was connected to the railway network in 1849.

The development of Eastbourne's sea front was relatively controlled, largely because most of the land belonged to only two individuals, the 7th Duke of Devonshire, and to a lesser extent, Carew Davis Gilbert. Between them, they were able to plan the wide thoroughfares, graceful stuccoed buildings and spacious gardens which characterise the town's three mile long esplanade. Among the noteworthy buildings constructed around this time are the handsome Regency-style Burlington Hotel, St Saviour's Church, the town hall, and the unusually elegant **railway station**. Eastbourne's classic seaside **pier** was built in 1880s and is one of the finest examples of its type in the country.

Despite its distinctive Victorian flavour, a settlement has existed on the site for many centuries. The remains of a Roman ship were discovered here in the 1960s, and the parish church of St Mary dates from around 1200. Other pre-Regency buildings include the flint and cobble built Old Rectory and the 13th century Lambe Inn in the High Street. A total of 14 Martello towers were built along the sea front in the early 19th century when a Napoleonic invasion seemed likely. One of these, the Wish Tower, has been restored and now houses the ***Coastal Defence Museum***, an interesting museum which chronicles Britain's attempts over the centuries to resist invasion from the sea. It can be found just to the west of the pier, approximately half way along the esplanade.

The circular ***Redoubt Tower*** in Royal Parade is another, even larger, Martello tower which has been converted for modern use. As well as containing an aquarium and the popular Treasure Island children's play centre, it is also the home of the Sussex Combined Services Museum, an informative museum on the history of Sussex based military units. The ***Royal National Lifeboat Museum*** lies on the sea front within a few yards of the Wish Tower; when it first opened in 1937, it was the first of its kind in the country.

Eastbourne has a proud reputation for its floral gardens and indeed, it would be hard to find a more typically English display of spring bulbs and summer bedding plants than here. The ***Carpet Gardens*** beside the pier have an international reputation and are one of the finest remaining examples of the art of carpet gardening, a style which first became popular in the 18th century. Both Helen Gardens, with their fine views along the cliffs to Beachy Head, and the Italian Gardens, a place much visited by George V and Queen Mary during their stay in 1935, can be found at Holywell, at the western end of the esplanade; Princes Park, at the opposite end, has a popular boating lake with rowing boats for hire; Hampden Park further inland incorporates a lake and bird sanctuary.

The acclaimed ***Towner Art Gallery and Local History Museum*** is housed in an 18th century manor house which also enjoys an attractive landscaped setting. It contains an impressive collection of work by 19th and 20th century British sculptors and painters, including Henry Moore, Elizabeth Frink and John Piper. An international women's tennis tournament takes place prior to Wimbledon each year on the celebrated grass courts of Devonshire Park, and the famous ***Grand Parade Bandstand*** on the front holds traditional brass and military band concerts throughout the year. Eastbourne's all-weather attractions include the Butterfly Centre on the promenade, the Sovereign pool and leisure complex, and the 'How We Lived Then' museum of shops in Cornfield Terrace.

A wonderful excursion from Eastbourne is to the summit of ***Beachy Head***, three miles west of the town centre. This magnificent white chalk cliff marks the eastern end of the South Downs and from the pleasant grassy picnicking area at the top, there's an almost sheer drop of well over 500 feet to the waves below. The views from here are superb: to the east it is possible to see as far as

Dungeness, to the west as far as Selsey Bill and the Isle of Wight, and to the south as far as the distant cargo ships which ply the busy shipping lanes of the English Channel.

The colossal mass of Beachy Head dwarfs the red and white banded lighthouse which stands on the wave-cut platform at its base. Notwithstanding, this distinctive granite built structure throws out a beam of light which can be seen over 15 miles out to sea. This stretch of coastline was once known as the 'Devil's Cape' because of its danger to shipping, and to this day the lighthouse has to continue its vital task of deterring ships from straying too close to the cliffs.

# Around Eastbourne

### Polegate                                            *Map 3 ref N8*
*4 miles NW of Eastbourne off the A22*

Here visitors will find the fascinating ***Polegate Windmill and Milling Museum***; built in 1817, it is the only tower windmill in Sussex open to the public. At the northeast edge of town, the remains of ***Otham Priory***, which was founded in 1175, now form part of a private house. The chapel can be seen from the part of the Cuckoo Line footpath that runs along the former railway track.

### Hailsham                                            *Map 3 ref N7*
*10 miles N of Eastbourne off the A22*

The market town of Hailsham was granted its Charter in 1252 by Henry III. Once a thriving centre of the string and rope industry, it boasts the fine St Mary the Virgin church, 13th century in origin but much altered, with a chequered flint pinnacled tower. ***Hailsham Heritage Centre*** contains an interesting collection of memorabilia, including a reconstruction of a Victorian kitchen.

### Upper Dicker                                        *Map 3 ref N7*
*10 miles NW of Eastbourne off the A22*

Upper Dicker is the site of one of the loveliest old monastic houses in Sussex, ***Michelham Priory***. This surprisingly well-preserved Augustinian priory was founded in 1229 by Gilbert de Aquila, the Norman lord of Pevensey, and continued to flourish until Henry VIII's Dissolution of the Monasteries in 1537. It then became the focal point of a large agricultural estate which for nearly three centuries belonged to the Sackville family.

The six acre priory site is situated on a small peninsula which is

**Michelham Priory**

surrounded on three sides by the River Cuckmere. The remaining side is separated from the mainland by a slow flowing moat whose water is still used to power an old mill where traditionally ground flour is produced in small batches to this day. Those entering the priory make their way across an old stone bridge and through a magnificent 14th century gatehouse. A number of other structures have been incorporated into the original monastic buildings over the centuries, including a large Elizabethan barn, a blacksmith's workshop, a wheelwright's shop, a rope museum and a Tudor wing which has been converted into an interesting exhibition area.

The priory grounds are beautifully laid out and include separate herbaceous, rose and evergreen borders; there is also an unusual physic garden which is planted with a variety of early medicinal herbs. The river and moat attract many different species of wild-fowl and other water loving birds throughout the year.

## Ripe
*Map 3 ref M7*

*12 miles NW of Eastbourne off the A22*

Here in the attractive community of Ripe, St John the Baptist Chuch contains several references to the local landed family, the Pelhams. There is also an exceptional building known as the Old Cottage which is faced with a remarkable set of wooden carvings.

## *Chiddingly* *Map 3 ref N6*
### *12 miles N of Eastbourne off the A22*

Chiddingly Church has a towering 128 foot stone spire which can be seen for miles around. From the churchyard, there are wonderful views in all directions and, inside, there is a monument to the Sir John Jefferay, Queen Elizabeth I's Chancellor of the Exchequer. The Jefferay family used to reside at nearby *Chiddingly Place*, a once splendid Tudor mansion which, sadly, is now in ruins; a large timber-framed barn from the same era has, however, been saved from dilapidation. Another Tudor residence which has managed to survive the ravages of time is Stonehill House, a mile and a half to the northeast.

## *East Hoathly* *Map 3 ref M6*
### *14 miles NW of Eastbourne off the A22*

Immortalised in Thomas Turners' 'Diary of East Hoathly', this handsome village has a chuch with a 15th century tower and a pre-Raphaelite inspired mural on the east wall of the chancel depicting the archangels Gabriel, Michael, Uriel and Raphael with a lamb.

Situated on the High Street in the pleasant village of East Hoathly, just opposite the home of 18th century diarist Thomas Turner, *Clara's gift shop and tearooms* occupies a lovely building dating back to the same period. Cheerful and hospitable owner Jane Seabrook offers fine teas and coffees and freshly baked cakes and savouries in warm and cosy country style surroundings. The

**Clara's Gift Shop and Tearooms**

shop stocks a range of tasteful antiques and gifts, cards and books, including a volume of Turner's writings on daily life in East Hoathly (1754-1765). Upstairs in the lovely beamed gallery there is a wide range of Rowan knitting yarn for sale along with a few select items of designer knitwear, and also a fascinating exhibition of traditional knitting and sewing implements. *Clara's, 9 High Street, East Hoathly, East Sussex BN8 6DR Tel: 01825 840339.*

## Around Uckfield

The scattered community of Uckfield is a thriving residential town which underwent a rapid development after it was joined to the rail network in the mid-19th century (although the line now terminates here, until the 1960s it continued on to Lewes). Thanks in part to the efforts of the Uckfield Preservation Society, a small number of buildings survive from the pre-railway period; these include the Georgian Maiden's Head Hotel, and Hook Hall, with its unusual chequered facade. Bridge Cottage is a fine example of a mediaeval hall house. The best way to explore Uckfield's history is to take the Uckfield Town Walk (details available from the Tourist Information Centre). During the 1980s the Society was also responsible for restoring nearby **Nutley Post** windmill to working order.

   **The Alma** pub in Uckfield is a handsome and imposing white-washed stone built pub dating back to the 1800s which has been in the same family for three generations. Owner Joy Hughes takes great pride in carrying on the tradition of friendly and hospitable service. This popular and traditional 'local' derives its name from

*The Alma*

the famous battle of the Crimean campaign - many local roads have also been named after this famous scene of conflict. A recent refurbishment has enhanced the pub's interior decor without taking anything away from its original Victorian features and ambience. In short, The Alma remains what it has always been: a comfortable, unpretentious pub offering a good selection of beers, wines and spirits, as well as hearty and well-prepared traditional bar meals. Joy Hughes is a friendly, welcoming host with an impressive knowledge of the local area and its history. Within walking distance of the centre of Uckfield, this agreeable establishment makes for a relaxing and congenial place to stop for a snack, drink and some pleasant conversation. *The Alma, Framfield Road, Uckfield, West Sussex TN22 5AJ Tel: 01825 762232 Fax: 01825 766173.*

**Barnsgate Manor Vineyard** 2 miles north of Uckfield at Herons Ghyll was established in the early 1970s. There are 12 acres of vines, 10 producing white grapes and two black. A map available from the on-site shop outlines a marked trail round the vineyard and grounds. Along the way you will come across the vineyard's resident donkeys, Buttercup, Dandelion and Heidi. Owner Linda Johnston also keeps a llama farm a few miles away, with woolly

***Barnsgate Manor Vineyard***

llamas and alpacas, some of which she brought over personally from South America. The Barnsgate wines produced in the on-site winery are available to taste or buy from the shop, which also features an unusual variety of gifts including Portmeiron pottery, basketware, preserves, chutneys and wine accessories. There is also an attractive tea room and restaurant, where you can lunch or dine on the patio enjoying the marvellous views. The vineyard (admission free), tea room and shop are open every day 10 a.m. till dusk; the restaurant is open every day for lunch from noon and for dinner on some evenings. *Barnsgate Manor Vineyard, Herons Ghyll, Nr Uckfield, East Sussex TN22 4DB Tel: 01825 713366 Fax: 01825 713543.*

## Isfield

*Map 3 ref L5*

*2 miles SW of Uckfield off the A26*

Isfield is known for the Lavender Line, part of the former Lewes to Uckfield line first opened in 1858, closed down in 1969, and joyfully restored to its former glory and decorated in the original Southern Railway colours and now maintained by the Lavender Line Preservation Society. Named after A E Lavender and Sons of Ringmer, the coal merchants who operated out of Isfield Station Yard, this wonderful working railway museum features vintage steam train rides, picnic area, and gift shop. Special 'footplate experience' days also available.

*The Laughing Fish* is a handsome, intimate public house and restaurant in this quiet, countryside village, near the Rivers Ouse and Uck, numerous country walks, and historic Lewes. Also convenient for Uckfield, Brighton and Eastbourne, this handsome establishment is popular with walkers, cyclists, anglers and visitors to the Lavender Line steam railway, next door. Originally the Station Hotel, the cosy interior boasts open fireplaces and long oak pews, and is decorated with fine prints of fishing and hunting scenes. Drag

*The Laughing Fish*

hunts still commence from the door. The Laughing Fish is famous for its club sandwiches; other treats on the menu include tasty brunches, trout, mixed grills, curry of the day and cheesy chips. The range of ales includes the unique and distinguished Beards Best Bitter. *The Laughing Fish, Station Road, Isfield, Nr Uckfield, East Sussex TN22 5XB Tel: 01825 750349.*

## Halland
*Map 3 ref M6*

*3 miles SE of Uckfield off the A22*

The renowned **Bentley Wildfowl and Motor Museum** is located near Halland. The estate covers some 100 acres in the heart of beautiful Sussex countryside and has something to spark everyone's interest.

**Bentley House** is a magnificent Palladian style mansion surrounded by lush green fields and woodland. An architectural masterpiece, this beautiful building started life as a Tudor farmhouse and has since been extended and sympathetically altered to create the splendid building you see today. Exquisitely furnished throughout, the house is particularly renowned for its Chinese room and the Philip Rickman gallery which houses a collection of over 150 of the Sussex artist's watercolours of wildfowl.

Outside, the formal gardens are similarly laid out to Bentley House, as a series of rooms, separated by hedges of yew and often themed by colour, for example, the blue garden. Exploring the grounds still further will lead you to Glyndebourne Wood, a cool tranquil place with conifers and various broad leaved trees providing shade between the sunny glades.

Bentley's Wildfowl Reserve boasts more than 150 different species, eleven of which are listed as endangered. Bentley Motor Museum is a must for motoring enthusiasts. Housing a magnificent collection of 50 cars and 25 motor bikes, ranging from veteran, Edwardian and vintage to modern day Lamborghini, many of the vintage models are regular participants in the London to Brighton run and some are very rare models indeed.

# CHAPTER FIVE
## The Cinque Ports & The East Sussex Coast

*Battle Abbey*

# Chapter 5 - Area Covered

*For precise location of places please refer to the colour maps found at the rear of the book.*

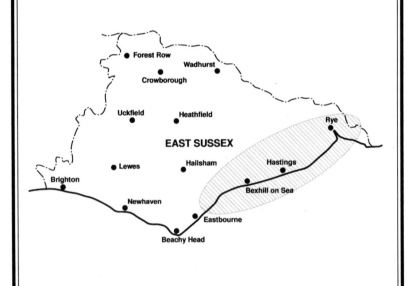

# 5

# *The Cinque Ports & The East Sussex Coast*

## Introduction

The story of this region of the East Sussex Coast is, of course, centred around the most famous date in English history: 1066. And the town of Hastings stakes perhaps the greatest claim on history as the scene, on 14th October 1066, of William the Conqueror's Norman invasion of England and defeat of King Harold in the Battle of Hastings (actually staged at the town of Battle, some six miles northwest). William's castle still stands on West Hill in Hastings as the city's foremost monument.

Long before even this, Hastings was a place of moment. By 928 the town had its own mint and in 1050 the town joined Romney, Hythe, Dover and Sandwich in the institution known as the *'Cinque Ports'*. The task of the Cinque Ports was to defend the Sussex and Kent coastline from attack. At one point Hastings supplied 20 of the 57 ships which made up the Cinque Ports navy - the only English navy in existence until the 15th century. These original five were later joined by Rye, Winchelsea, Pevensey and other towns along the coast (some of which are now several miles inland, due in part to the strong southwesterly winds and sea currents which carried enormous quantities of sand and shingle, cutting them off from the sea).

Many other locations speak of a rich and ancient past, such as Pevensey with its ruined castle. And, quite apart from a rich history, the region offers many modern-day delights in the coastal re-

sorts of St Leonards and Bexhill-on-Sea, the charming and picturesque town of Rye, and the famous gardens at Great Dixter. With
handsome architecture dating from mediaeval times through to the
present day, gorgeous scenes of natural beauty, the area's multitude
of sights, sounds and spectacles make it well worth a visit.

## Bexhill-on-Sea

In common with most other seaside resorts on the Channel coast,
Bexhill was not much more than a fishing and smuggling community before the arrival of the railway in the 19th century. A good
number of pre-Victorian features have managed to survive, including the old weather-boarded cottages and commercial buildings in
Church Street, the 14th century Manor House, and the part Norman parish church of St Peter , which stands on the site of an ancient Neolithic earthwork.

Modern Bexhill owes its character to the local landed family, the
Earls De la Warr, who developed the town in the 1880s. (Many
years before, a branch of the family had an influence in the naming
of the American state of Delaware.) Most of the features characteristic of an English seaside resort date from this late Victorian period, including the promenade and the floral gardens in *Egerton
Park*. *Bexhill Museum* on the edge of Egerton Park houses an
interesting collection of artefacts pertaining to the natural history,
geology and archaeology of the area. *The Manor Gardens* in the
old town contain an aviary, open-air theatre, walled garden and the
renowned *Museum of Costume and Social History*. This unique
collection of historic costumes is arranged in a series of imaginative
settings covering the period from 1740s to the 1940s.

Perhaps the most striking feature of the town, however, wasn't
built until the 1930s. The *De la Warr Pavilion* was designed by
the acclaimed architects Mendelsohn and Chermayeff in a style reminiscent of an ocean-going liner, and contains a theatre, concert hall,
ballroom and elegant terrace bar. Now Grade I listed, it attracts an
international line-up of performing artists throughout the year.

*The Nelson Guest House*, owned by Ian McElroy, nestles on a
quiet street behind the centre of Bexhill on Sea, only a few minutes'
walk from the railway station and all of the town's attractions
stretched out along the seafront. The modest white-fronted exterior
and the tranquil location disguise the fact that the Nelson is Bexhill's
largest guest house. Broad hallways link the nine well-proportioned
rooms which, like the guest house itself, combine spaciousness with

**The Nelson Guest House**

homeliness. A large parking area and beautiful garden behind the house looks out on the hills backing the town. Some of the guests have no need for the car park, since the Nelson is popular with ramblers who appreciate the ample rooms and fortifying breakfasts. Ian is a rambler of a different sort, having moved to Sussex from London some years ago to run his first guest house in Eastbourne before making the move to Bexhill. *Nelson Guest House, 6 Station Road, Bexhill on Sea, East Sussex TN40 1RE Tel: 01424 214063.*

At very low tides a submerged forest reveals itself on the beach, evidence that the coastline has changed dramatically over the centuries. To find this hidden forest, cross the sand and shingle from the foot of Galley Hill.

Bexhill was the first resort to allow mixed bathing on its beaches in 1900, and was regarded as very progressive in its day; today it is more the domain of the traditional. Nevertheless, the gently sloping shingle beaches offer clean and safe bathing, and there are also good facilities for windsurfing and other watersports.

In many ways Bexhill is a rarity: a south coast seaside town that has remained relatively peaceful and serene. Having recently acquired the ***Buenos Aires*** guest house, owners Susannah and Mark Snell have lavished great thoughtfulness and care on turning it into a homely and charming traditional B&B. Their hard work has paid off, and continues to do so: they have made this establishment a welcoming haven of peace and comfort. Visitors return again and again, knowing they will receive the best in hospitality and friendly, helpful service and attention. Open all year round, this attractive and roomy B&B makes the ideal place for an early or late season break. The rooms are spotless and decorated with great care and consideration for guests' every comfort. Ideally situated within a few strides of the sea front, and only steps away from the diversions offered by Bexhill, guests here can look forward to hearty full English breakfasts and, if requested, evening meals as well. *Buenos Aires, 24 Albany Road, Bexhill-on-Sea, East Sussex TN4 1BZ Tel: 01424 212269.*

***Buenos Aires Guest House***

# Around Bexhill

## *Pevensey*                                         *Map 4 ref O8*
### *4 miles SW of Bexhill off the A259*

The low lying land around Pevensey proved a good landing place for the invading Roman legions, and in order to protect their strategic anchorage, the Romans erected a massive fortification (they went on to build 10 such strongholds along the southern shores of Britain). Although **Pevensey Castle** now lies almost two miles inland, it once stood on the shoreline within a few yards of the Roman landing stages. The steady eastward drift of the shingle beach gradually isolated Pevensey from the English Channel, a process which was inadvertently accelerated by the draining of the Pevensey Levels during Tudor times.

In 1066, the invading forces of William the Conqueror also landed in Pevensey Bay and used the castle to billet his troops prior to the Battle of Hastings. Then, after the Norman Conquest, the surrounding lands were granted to the Count of Mortain, who constructed a smaller fortification within the original Roman ramparts using stone from the earlier structure. Two centuries later this castle successfully resisted a siege by Simon de Montfort's forces, attempting to oust the supporters of Henry III following the Battle of Lewes in 1264. The structure then gradually fell into disrepair as it became increasingly isolated from the sea, although it was briefly reoccupied at around the time of the Spanish Armada, and again during the Second World War. The ruins of Pevensey Castle are now under the ownership of English Heritage.

As can be seen, from its Roman origins to its involvement in the Second World War, Pevensey Castle has played an important role in history. Visitors can take an audio tour to find out about the castle's early origins - including its famous visitor in 1066 - and explore this medieval ruin complete with dungeons! There is also the castle tea room, open for light lunches or afternoon tea. Open daily 1st April - 31st October 10-6 (or dusk in October); Wednesday - Sunday 1st November - 31st March 10-4 (closed 24th-26th December). Admission charge. Featured events include Robin Hood Plays and exhibitions of Roman and Norman painting and pottery. *English Heritage Tel: 01323 762604.*

The village of Pevensey contains an unusual number of fine mediaeval buildings, including the *Mint House*, built in the 1340s on the site of a Norman mint, and the *Court House*, which served the borough as a combined courtroom and gaol; both buildings now house interesting museums of local history. There are also a number of excellent old inns in the village, and *Glyndley Manor*, on the edge of Pevensey, renowned for its mysterious atmosphere and celebrated colony of herons.

In the days prior to the founding of the Royal Navy, Pevensey served as one of the nation's Cinque Ports - that is to say, it was granted certain privileges by the Crown in return for providing ships and men in defence of the Channel coast. Several centuries later, a series of *Martello Towers* was built along the coast to the east of Pevensey to defend the shore against a possible attack from the forces of Napoleon.

Inland lies the area of drained marshland known as the *Pevensey Levels*. At one time this was an area of tidal mud flats which were covered in shallow salt pans; since then, however, it has been reclaimed for agricultural use and is now covered in fertile arable fields.

## Ninfield                                      *Map 4 ref P6*
*4 miles NW of Bexhill off the A271*

This sprawling village is home to the little Church of St Mary the Virgin, which retains its mediaeval lancet windows. Approached through a tunnel of trees, this fine church features a delightful 19th century clock mechanism inside.

## St Leonards                                   *Map 4 ref Q7*
*3 miles E of Bexhill off the A259*

St Leonards was founded in the 1820s as a fashionable seaside resort. It was created by James Burton, the celebrated London architect who was responsible for designing much of Bloomsbury. With the assistance of his son, Decimus, a talented architect in his own right who went on to design the Wellington Arch at Hyde Park Corner in London, he created a model seaside town which was designed to attract the wealthy and aristocratic.

The focus of regency St Leonards is the ***Royal Victoria Hotel*** on the seafront, a handsome stuccoed brick building which was designed in classical style with a broad pedimented facade. The low colonnade on either side of the hotel creates a striking formal promenade. ***Crown House***, Burton's original seaside residence, was given to Princess (later Queen) Victoria when she visited St Leonards in 1834.

In its heyday, the resort's formal social activities took place in the Assembly Rooms (now the Masonic Hall), a building which was connected by tunnel to the hotel kitchens so that provisions could be brought in for social functions. The delightfully informal ***St Leonards Gardens*** stand a little inland from here. Originally private gardens maintained by the subscriptions of local residents, they were acquired by the local authority in 1880 and now provide a delightfully tranquil area with lakes, mature trees and gently sloping lawns. The gardens also contain a number of fine Regency buildings, including the Clock House, which appears to be three storeys high from the park but only one from the road behind, Allegria Court, Burton's former home, and Gloucester Lodge, the former residence of Princess Sophia of Gloucester.

***North Lodge***, a castellated gatehouse to the north of the park, was built to guard the northern entrance to the town. It was also once the home of Sir Henry Rider Haggard, the author of *King Solomon's Mines* and other classic adventure stories.

Victorian St Leonards even had its own service areas: ***Mercatoria***, the tradesmen's quarter, and ***Lavatoria***, the laundry-women's quarter. ***Burton's Tomb***, the curious pyramid shaped vault where James Burton and several member of his family were buried, can be found in the grounds of the old parish church in West Hill.

Guided walking tours of this fascinating resort are available regularly; there is also a detailed written guide at local bookshops and the Tourist Information Centre.

### *Ashburnham*                                              *Map 4 ref P6*
*6 miles NW of Bexhill off the B2096*
The hamlet of Ashburnham is a truly hidden place which lies in the country lanes between the hamlets of Penhurst and Ponts Green. One of the last surviving centres of the Sussex iron industry, a sizable foundry operated here for around three centuries until the beginning of the 19th century. The old foundry buildings are still in existence, along with the remains of the great hammer ponds which once channelled water to the mechanical hammers and bellows.

***Ashburnham Forge*** stands on the northern edge of the privately owned ***Ashburnham Park***, a 1,000 acre country estate which was landscaped by Capability Brown in the 18th century. One of his finest creations is the series of artificial lakes which he constructed in the shallow valley in front of ***Ashburnham Place***. The church within the grounds contains a number of fine monuments to the Ashburnham family.

# Hastings

Long before William the Conqueror made his well publicised landing on the beaches of nearby Pevensey Bay, Hastings was the principal town of a small semi-independent Saxon province which straddled the Kent-Sussex border. By the mid 10th century it was an important port and even had its own mint. Following the Battle of Hastings, which in fact took place six miles inland at the place now called Battle, the Normans chose a promontory to the west of the old town to build their first stone castle in England. Sections of the north and east walls, a gatehouse, tower and dungeons still remain, and the stiff walk up to the castle site is rewarded with some magnificent views of the town and surrounding coastline.

Over the centuries, Hastings has been subjected to periodic attack from the sea, both from cross Channel raids, which on at least one occasion left the town a smouldering ruin, and from the waves themselves, which would regularly flood the streets during stormy conditions. The town's busy fishing harbour started to silt up during the Elizabethan era and now lies buried beneath a 20th century shopping development. Nevertheless, the fishing industry managed to survive and, today, fishing vessels continue to be hoisted onto the shingle beach by motor winch. One of Hastings' most characteristic features are the tall, narrow wooded huts which are used for for dying nets and storing fishing tackle; these date from the 17th century and are known as *net shops* or *deezes*. The old fishermen's church of St Nicholas now houses the **Fishermen's Museum**, an interesting exhibition which includes the full-sized sailing lugger, *Enterprise*. This was the last vessel to be built in Hastings before the shipyard closed in 1909; it was actively involved in the Dunkirk evacuation of 1940.

The old part of Hastings consists of a network of narrow streets and alleyways, or *twittens*, which lie between Castle Hill and East Hill. The best way discover the many interesting old residential buildings, inns and churches is to take a walking tour along the High Street and All Saints Street. (Those especially interested in churches should follow the 'Hastings Church Trail', a pleasant walk which takes in seven churches, most of them mediaeval.) **St Clement's Church** in the High Street has two cannonballs embedded in its tower, one of which was fired from a French warship, and the **Stag Inn** in All Saints Street has a concealed entrance to a smugglers' secret passage and a pair of macabre 400 year old mummified cats.

There are two cliff railways in Hastings, one on each side of the old town. The West Hill railway runs underground and carries passengers up to Hastings Castle, the lighthouse and the famous St Clement's Caves.

**Hastings Castle** is forever linked with that most famous date in English history - 1066. The ruins of William the Conqueror's 900 year old castle stand on the West Hill cliff edge commanding panoramic views. It is also the home of *'The 1066 Story'*. Here, from within a medieval siege tent, an audio-visual presentation transports visitors back in time, recounting the history of the castle.

From the Castle, it's only a short walk across the West Hill to another great experience - **Smugglers Adventure**. This will really set your imagination alive. You descend into the winding tunnels and caverns of St. Clements Caves to explore the secret passages on a journey through time. You can relive the dangers and excitements of the smugglers and Customs men and witness the romantic and often bloody heyday of the smuggler. The themed experience includes a museum of smuggling, a video theatre and subterranean adventure walk where you will discover more than 50 life-size figures, scenes activated by push buttons, dramatic sounds, eerie lighting and a few unexpected surprises! For access to both Smugglers Adventure & The 1066 Story, follow signs to the car park on the beach at Pelham Place and take the West Hill Railway to the top of the West Hill.

Hastings also contains a variety of attractions for the traditional seaside holidaymaker. The 600 foot long *Pier* was completed in 1872 and had to be repaired after the Second World War when it was deliberately holed in two places to prevent it being used as a landing stage by Hitler's forces. According to local legend, the Conqueror's Stone at the head of the pier was used by William the Conqueror as a dining table for his first meal on English soil in 1066.

Eighty one events spanning 900 years of the town's history are remembered in the impressive *Hastings Embroidery* in the town hall. Inspired by the Bayeux Tapestry, this remarkable 240ft long embroidery was made by the Royal School of Needlework in 1966 to commemorate the ninth centenary of the Norman Invasion. Among the characters to be depicted is John Logie Baird, the Scottish pioneer of television who carried out his early experiments here in the 1920s.

The 600 acre *Hastings Country Park* to the east of the town offers some spectacular clifftop walking along two and a half miles of unspoilt coastline. Guided walks through this attractive area of woodland and heath are provided by the local ranger service throughout the summer.

## Around Hastings

**Battle**                                                    *Map 4 ref Q6*
*5 miles NW of Hastings off the A2100*

The historic settlement of Battle is of course renowned as the location of the momentous battle on 14th October 1066 between the forces of Harold, the Saxon King of England, and William, Duke of Normandy. The Battle of Hastings actually took place on a hill which the Normans named Senlac, meaning lake of blood - even today, some believe in the myth that blood seeps from the battlefield after heavy rain (any discolouring of the water is, in fact, due to iron oxide in the subsoil).

**Battle Abbey**

The High Street in Battle is a long road with plenty to occupy the passing tourist or local. Prior to 1066, the site of Battle was virtually uninhabited; however, one of William the Conqueror's first tasks on becoming King of England was to found a substantial Benedictine abbey on this exposed hillside in order to make amends for the loss of life in battle and so secure his future salvation. St Martin's Abbey was finally consecrated in 1094, the high altar in the great church being placed on the very spot where Harold was struck in the eye by an arrow from a Norman bow.

Throughout the late Middle Ages, the abbey grew wealthy and powerful as it extended its influence over a wide area of East Sussex. This period of prosperity came to an abrupt end, however, following Henry VIII's Dissolution of the Monasteries in 1537. Several of the old monastic buildings are open to visitors, including the towering 13th century dormitory and the monks' common room with its magnificent vaulted ceiling. The mile long *'Battlefield Walk'* guides visitors around the edge of Senlac Hill and describes the course of the battle with the help of models and information boards, while the imposing 14th century gatehouse contains an exhibition which brings the history of the abbey to life.

Under the auspices of English Heritage, the *1066 Battle of Hastings and Abbey ruins* exhibition allows visitors to discover thrilling facts behind the most famous date in English history, at the very site of the battle and its nearby Abbey. This exciting exhibition helps visitors experience what led up to that fateful day. Open daily 1st April - 31st October daily 10-6 (or dusk in October); daily 1st November - 31st March 10-4 . Last wand issued 1 hour before closing. Admission charge. Featured events for all the family include spectacular battle re-enactments, music and drama, sheepdog and falconry displays, classic car shows, Bayeux Tapestry Final. Tel: 01424 773792. *English Heritage, Battle Abbey, Battle, East Sussex TN33 0AD, Tel. 01424 775705.*

Battle offers a number of other noteworthy attractions, apart from the battle site and Abbey. The parish church of St Mary the Virgin, for example, was built early in the 12th century and, like many of its contemporaries, was restored by the Victorians. Inside, there is an unusual covered Norman font, some fine stained glass windows, a fascinating wall painting, the early Renaissance Tomb of Sir Anthony Browne and a memorial to Sir Edward Cartwright, inventer of the power looms dating back to the 13th century. The *Battle Museum of Local History* in Langton House contains a half-size reproduction of the Bayeux Tapestry, a facsimile of the Sussex volume of the Domesday Book, and an interesting collection of old maps, coins, toys and games.

Just opposite Battle Abbey, in 600 year old Wealden Hall House, you will find *Buckleys Yesterday's World* - a collection of around 100,000 historic artefacts and items of memorabilia dating from Victorian and Edwardian times right up until 1950. A number of good small shops and inns can be found in the High Street and the old market place, and in summer there are historic re-enactments, archery displays, and many other festivities.

## Hooe

*Map 4 ref P7*

*7 miles W of Hastings off the B3029*

The village of Hooe stretches along a low ridge looking towards the sea over the Pevensey Levels. There is a handsome green, Hooe Common, at the northern edge of the village. The mostly 15th century St Oswald's Church, isolated above the fields some way out of the village, has a chancel of the type known as 'weeping' because it is set at an angle to the nave, in a way meant to represent the angle of Christ's head on the cross.

Originally two small country cottages built in the 15th century, the **Lamb Inn** was granted a pub licence by the Abbott of Battle in 1510 - a licence given with the stipulation that the pub remain open day and night during lambing season, as a place for shepherds to come in from the cold. The present buildings comprise the old pub and the stables, restored in the early 19th century and sympathetically restored in recent times. The handsome open-plan interior

**The Lamb Inn**

boasts open fires, exposed oak beams and uprights, low wheel-type chandeliers and festoons of dried flowers, all adding to the warm and welcoming ambience. This historic, traditional establishment on the Pevensey Levels - some two miles from Hooe, a manor once the property of Harold II, killed at the battle of Hastings - can boast real character and a convivial atmosphere, to accompany the fine ales and excellent range of meals and snacks. This ancient hostelry proudly upholds the traditions of the classic country pub, a reputation that the staff work hard to maintain, with great success. *Lamb Inn, Sewerbridge, Hooe, Nr Battle, East Sussex TN33 9HH Tel. 01424 847891*.

## Brede

*Map 4 ref R.*

*6 miles N of Hastings off the A28*

The village of Brede has a history shrouded in myth and tales of the supernatural. The legend of the Brede Giant is based around the 16th century figure of Sir Goddard Oxenbridge, by all accounts a normal, God fearing member of society except for his unusual height - over 7 foot tall. Some time after his death, the story spread that he had been a terrible child-devouring monster who was eventually done away with by a band of vengeful children who fed him strong ale and then cut him in half using a two-handled wooden saw

Oxenbridge's remains lie in a tomb in St George's Church, but his ghost is still said to haunt his 15th century family home, **Brede Place**.

## Sedlescombe
*Map 4 ref Q5*

*6 miles N of Hastings off the A229*

The delightful village of Sedlescombe, a former iron-founding settlement, is stretched out along a long, gently sloping green with a part 14th century church (St John the Baptist) at the top and a pillared pump house built in 1900 near the bottom. The brick and tile-hung houses lining the green are mostly 16th and 17th century, and there are also a couple of good hostelries, the Brickwall Hotel and **The Queen's Head**, a fine old coaching house dating back to the 1520s. Still the traditional meeting place for the local hunt, this

**The Queen's Head**

grand public house - with its tile roof and leaded windows, large inglenook fireplace (the fire-back in the bar is dated 1754), vast collection of Toby jugs, horse harnesses on the walls and dried hops, tankards and old drinking vessels hanging from the exposed ceiling beams - is every inch the traditional country pub.

The atmosphere is friendly and relaxing; on offer is a very good selection of beers and malt whiskies, as well as tasty bar snacks and sandwiches. Near the historic towns of Battle, some 3 miles away, and Hastings, this handsome establishment, under the ownership of the amiable John and Jackie Cook, offers fine potables in peaceful and charming surroundings. *The Queen's Head, Sedlescombe, East Sussex TN33 0QA Tel: 01424 870228.*

The internationally renowned **Pestalozzi Children's Village** is situated on a country estate to the southeast of Sedlescombe. It was founded in 1959 to carry on the work of the 19th century Swiss educational reformer, Johann Heinrich Pestalozzi, on the premise that young people of all nationalities should learn together. The village now specialises in educating children from the Third World in the belief that their newly learnt skills will help them contribute to the development of their home countries.

## Robertsbridge
*9 miles NW of Hastings off the A21*

*Map 4 ref Q4*

Robertsbridge is an attractive village with weatherboarded cottages and shops, and inns built in mellow brick. Long associated with the manufacture of cricket bats, the village establishment Grey Nicholls has made cricket bats for some of the world's cricketing legends, including W G Grace.

Here in Robertsbridge, and originally a coaching house built in the 1800s, the ***New Eight Bells*** is a charming and popular village pub run by Tracy and Tom O'Neill and Tracy's mother, Kathy. Originally from Tilbury, Essex, they bought the pub in March 1997 and, with four young boys and their large, friendly German shepherd, they have created a very warm and hospitable atmosphere. A Free House, the Eight Bells serves a variety of guest beers. The base for this small community's Rugby Club, and home to their own pool, darts and shovepenny teams, there is a vast collection of sporting trophies on display, as well as a handsome selection of brassware,

***The New Eight Bells***

tankards, ornaments and bellows. Other interior features include wrought ironwork over the bar, black-beamed ceilings throughout and two open brick and tile surround fireplaces. The walls are adorned with signed rugby shirts, pictures of local teams, wildlife prints and cigarette card collection prints. The delicious food on offer is all home-cooked, the ingredients bought locally from the village butcher. Booking for Sunday lunch advised; special rates for senior citizens weekday lunchtimes. The completely refurbished function room can be booked for all occasions, including wedding parties. *New Eight Bells, Northbridge Street, Robertsbridge, East Sussex TN32 5NP Tel: 01580 880722.*

## Bodiam                                    Map 4 ref Q4
*10 miles N of Hastings off the A229*
Bodiam is home to the impressive National Trust-owned **Bodiam Castle**. With its imposing stone walls, castellated turrets and lily-filled moat, this must be the epitome of a classic romantic castle.

**Bodiam Castle**

Bodiam was one of the last great mediaeval fortifications to be built in Britain; it was constructed in 1385 by Sir Edward Dalyngrigge to defend the upper Rother valley against possible attack from the French following the infamous cross-Channel raid on Rye eight years before. The castle was very well-appointed for its day, but never saw hostile fire until nearly three centuries later, when the Parliamentarian forces of General Waller reduced it to a shell to avoid it becoming a Royalist stronghold during the English Civil War.

A long period of decay then followed until in 1829, plans to completely dismantle the castle were thwarted by 'Mad' Jack Fuller of Brightling. A programme of external restoration was begun by George Cubitt towards the end of the 19th century and completed by Lord Curzon, a former Viceroy of India, between 1917 and 1919. On his death in 1926, Curzon bequeathed Bodiam to the National Trust, who have carried on the process of restoration and conservation. Several floors in the towers have now been replaced, enabling visitors to climb to the top of the battlements. The castle hosts a number of events during the year, ranging from mediaeval archery and longbow competitions to family fun days.

On the southern side of the River Rother three quarters of a mile south of Bodiam, is a completely different place of interest called **Quarry Farm**, a 200 acre open farm which offers an entertaining day out for those with an interest in rural life. As well as a wide assortment of farm animals, there is an exhibition on the farmer's year, a collection of steam traction engines and a children's adventure play area.

## Northiam                                    *Map 4 ref R4*
*10 miles N of Hastings off the A28*

Northiam is a large and picturesque village which is known for its characteristic white weatherboarded buildings. At the heart of the community is a sizable village green which is surrounded by a number of fine 17th and 18th century buildings. Perhaps the most impressive of these is a substantial three storey white-boarded house which stands on the edge of the green behind an unusual carved stone monument.

Elizabeth I is reputed to have rested under the branches of Northiam's great oak whilst journeying to Rye in August 1573 (the tree is now believed to be over 1,000 years old). Her green high-heeled shoes must have been particularly uncomfortable, for she left them behind, magnanimously donating to the villagers who saved them as a memento of her brief royal visit (they can be seen at **Brickwall House**).

Northiam contains a surprising number of well preserved late-mediaeval buildings, including Strawberry Hole Farmhouse, Silverden Manor, Wellhouse and the Hayes Arms Hotel. The nave and chancel of **St Mary's Parish Church** were built of ironstone in the 14th century, and the tower has an unusual turreted staircase and a stone built spire, a feature rarely found in Sussex. Inside, there is an impressive mid 19th century mausoleum dedicated to the Frewen family, the local rectors and lords of the manor who lived at nearby Brickwall House. This imposing 17th century residence is noted for its fine plasterwork ceilings and stands within beautiful grounds which contain a chess garden, a rare early 18th century bowling alley, a sunken topiary garden and a charming formal garden with an unusually grand entrance.

One 17th century member of the Frewen family was a strict Puritan who named his two sons 'Accepted' and 'Thankful'. Accepted went on to become president of Magdalen College, Oxford and then the Archbishop of York, and Thankful is remembered for having donated the communion rails to the church in 1683.

The southern terminus of the Kent and East Sussex Railway can be found on the A28, a mile to the north of the village. Restored in 1990, steam trains run from here to Tenterden in Kent throughout the summer. At one time, the nearby River Rother was navigable to this point and barges were brought upstream to be unloaded at the busy quay. This practice must have gone on for centuries, for in 1822 the remains of a 60 foot Viking long ship were discovered in the mud beside the river, where they had lain since the 9th century.

***Great Dixter***, one of the finest examples of a late mediaeval hall-house, can be found three quarters of a mile to the northwest of Northiam. This superb building dates from around 1450 and was bought in 1911 by the architectural historian, Nathaniel Lloyd, after it had been on the market for ten years. Lloyd commissioned his friend, Edwin Lutyens, to remodel the house and he immediately set to work restoring the great hall and solar. Lutyens' stroke of genius was to incorporate a 16th century timbered house which he

***Great Dixter***

and Lloyd discovered eight miles away in Benenden, in Kent. The building, which had previously been covered in corrugated iron and used as a barn, was carefully re-erected alongside the original manor house and combined with it to form a single residence of delightful proportions. Part oak-timbered and part tile-hung, Great Dixter is now furnished with a carefully chosen collection of antique furniture, tapestries and oriental carpets.

When Lutyens was also asked to lay out the gardens at Great Dixter he came up with a truly imaginative design which retained several existing outbuildings and introduced a number of exciting new features, including a sunken garden, topiary lawn, orchards, horse pond and meadow garden. The estate is still in the hands of the Lloyd family, the gardens being the responsibility of Christopher Lloyd, the celebrated gardening writer and historian. Many rare and unusual plants are on sale to the public at Great Dixter's own nursery.

### Fairlight
*Map 4 ref S6*

*2 miles E of Hastings off the A259*

**White Cottage**, a welcoming B&B owned by John and June Dyer, lies at the outskirts of the pretty village of Fairlight, between Rye and Hastings. A distinctive eyebrow-shaped dormer window looks down at the spacious parking area to the front of the house, which is set in extensive gardens featuring benches, ponds, wildflowers and the occasional badger or fox feeding at night. There are panoramic views of the Channel from parts of the garden - and from some of the spacious guest rooms inside. The large breakfast room looks out on the garden and to the sea beyond. The Dyers are enthu-

**White Cottage**

siastic hosts, eager to tell guests about their collection of oil lamps and china or about the sights in nearby Rye, Hastings, Battle and Winchelsea. Their own village, Fairlight, is an attraction in itself, with attractive coves, clifftop walks and (on a clear day) a view of the French coast from the tower of the village church. *White Cottage, Battery Hill, Fairlight, East Sussex TN35 4AP  Tel: 01424 812528 Fax: 01424 812285.*

# Rye

Along with its neighbour to the southwest, Rye was added to the five existing Cinque Ports of Hastings, Romney, Hythe, Dover and Sandwich in the 12th century. The town was also subjected to ferocious cross Channel raids - almost every non stone built structure in the town was burnt to the ground in the notorious French raid of 1377. Later, the harbour suffered from the problems of a receding coastline, a dilemma which eventually required the building of a new port, Rye Harbour, closer to the repositioned mouth of the River Rother.

*Cobbles Tea Rooms*

Of course, Rye is a great place to wander around in, and home to a number of excellent places to stop for refreshment. **Cobbles Tea Rooms** is one such place, located in a charming former cottage, now transformed into a two room cafe, approached along a short, narrow path leading from its own whitewashed fence and gate and set in a true cottage garden with hanging baskets, climbers and a cobblestone path leading to the door. There's a table for two outside, or if you prefer (or the weather is not kind) you can make yourself comfortable inside, where all is neat, crisp and clean - a warm and cosy haven filled with delicious scents, the epitome of the English tea room. Everything on offer is home-made: cakes, pies, light lunches, quiche, and soups - and all of it delicious. And to drink? A fine selection of teas and freshly ground coffees, of course. Cream teas are a speciality - friendly and welcoming owners Jennafer and Rodney Hall create thousands of them every year. Located right in the centre of Rye, you may find yourself, like many of the other patrons, returning again and again for the warm hospitality and excellent food and drink. Open seven days a week. *Cobbles Tea Rooms, 1 Hylands Yard, Rye, East Sussex TN31 7EP Tel: 01797 225962.*

Rye's prominent hilltop site is partially ringed by the rivers Rother, Brede and Tillingham, a factor which has made it an easily defendable hill fort since early times. A substantial perimeter wall was built to defend the open northern approaches, and one of its four great gateways, the **Landgate**, still survives in the northeastern corner of the old town. This imposing 14th century structure once had oak gates, a drawbridge and a portcullis. The clock was added in 1863 in memory of Prince Albert, and was restored at the time of the Royal Wedding in 1981.

Rye grew prosperous in the late mediaeval period due to the activities of its fishing and merchant fleets, who brought in fish and cloth and sent out wool and processed iron to continental Europe. However, the silting up of the harbour gradually denied the town a means of earning a living and heralded a lengthy period of decline. This economic downturn halted the process of organic change in Rye and many of the buildings which would have been updated in more prosperous circumstances remained unchanged.

As a result, present day Rye has inherited a superb legacy of late-mediaeval buildings, most of which have been restored in the years since the town was 'rediscovered' in the 19th century. The local council now publishes an informative walking guide of the old town which is available from the public library or the bookshop in the High Street.

**Martello Bookshop** takes its name from the Martello towers, an important local feature of the coastal landscape in East Sussex. Books have been sold at this site in the centre of Rye since the 1890s. Once also a circulating library (2d. per volume per week), it was renovated in 1976, at which time the original shopfront's position on the pavement was reinstated (after 47 years), to a design by award winning local architects Lefevre, Wood and Royle. Specialising in art books, the shop also has a good range of paperback fiction and books on crafts, cookery, gardening, sports, wildlife and local history as well as reference books, children's books and maps. Rye has in its time been home to many important literary figures, including Henry James, Rumer Godden and E F Benson - whose Mapp and Lucia novels are all set in Rye. The bookshop publishes local poet Patric Dickinson's *Poems from Rye*, as well as a book entitled *E F Benson Remembered* by former owners Cynthia and Tony Reavell, who sold the shop to present owners Terry and Wendy Harvey in 1996. *Martello Bookshop, 26 High Street, Rye, East Sussex TN31 7JJ Tel: 01797 222242 Fax: 01797 227335.*

***Martello Bookshop***

While in the High Street, the pretty crimson coloured doorway with its panes of multicoloured glass above the frontage tells you that you have arrived at *Cranberries of Rye*, one of Rye's most distinguished tea rooms. Open seven days a week for morning tea or coffee, a light lunch or traditional cream tea, this very welcoming establishment is run with enthusiasm by owners Hilary and Ray Jones. Everything on the menu is home-made - some to customers' orders: scones, tea cakes, pastries, fruit cake, lemon cake, treacle tart, chocolate cake and meringues are just some of the delectables on offer, as well as soups, fresh

***Cranberries of Rye***

breads, and fresh or toasted sandwiches with a choice of fillings. To accompany these delicious comestibles there's an excellent choice of coffees and teas, as well as fruited teas, soft drinks and hot chocolate. Jams, marmalades, pickles, chutneys, honeys and cordials are on sale, as well as good quality hand-made teapots. *Cranberries of Rye, 105a High Street, Rye, East Sussex TN31 7JE Tel: 01797 224800.*

Down a narrow street in the centre of Rye, **The Union Inn** is a charming establishment dating back to the 15th century that looks for all the world just what it is: a charming, cosy and historic town pub. The whitewashed stone walls, casement windows and lanterns that adorn the exterior give you a flavour of what's to come. Inside, the atmosphere is relaxed and welcoming. Show cases line the walls, displaying a fine collection of fascinating militaria. There is also a handsome display of finely etched line drawings of RAF VC holders.

*The Union Inn*

Owner Steve Dartnell is the friendly and diverting host, a fount of interesting and amusing stories, as well as being very knowledgeable on military matters and history. A Free House offering a wide choice of beers and also real ales, with an excellent and extensive menu for meals and snacks, The Union is a very popular haunt with locals and visitors alike - booking is essential. *The Union Inn, East Street, Rye, East Sussex TN31 7JY Tel: 01797 222334.*

For luncheons, morning coffee or afternoon tea, try visiting **Fletchers Tea Rooms** in the heart of Rye. These very old established tea rooms in the shadow of the magnificent church on Lion Street offer famous cream teas and a choice of delicious light lunches and luscious pies, cakes, pastries and savouries. The tea rooms take their name from one John Fletcher, a 16th century dramatist and friend and aide to William Shakespeare. Fletcher lived here in this

**Fletchers Tea Rooms**

superb timber-framed house until his death in 1570. Owner Geraldine Bromley has many years' experience of catering to and pleasing her many customers, and they return the compliment by returning again and again for the hospitable service, cosy surroundings and excellent edibles. Geraldine makes a particularly wonderful - and renowned - fruit cake, to enjoy with one of the selection of fine teas and coffees on offer, or to purchase and savour at another time. *Fletchers Tea Rooms, Lion Street, Rye, East Sussex TN31 7LB Tel: 01797 223101.*

On your wanderings you will undoubtedly come to **Mermaid Street**, one of the finest examples of an unspoilt mediaeval thoroughfare in Rye. This delightful cobbled lane is lined with early timbered buildings including the famous Mermaid Inn, a wonderful old hostelry which was rebuilt in 1420 following the devastating

French raid of 43 years before. In the 18th century, the inn became the headquarters of the Hawkhurst Gang, one of the most infamous and powerful bands of smugglers on the south coast. Local legend has it that they always sat with their pistols at the ready in case of a sudden excisemen's raid. A series of events recording the inn's past are displayed on boards at the front of the building.

**The Mermaid Street Coffee House** takes its name from this, one of Rye's most famous cobbled streets, lined with houses up to 500 years old. It stands at the top of Mermaid Street, with hanging baskets framing the distinctive bow-fronted double doors that follow the curve of the street. Mrs Julie Bryant, the owner, saw this lovely setting as the fulfilment of a dream to open a quaint coffee

**The Mermaid Street Coffee House**

house. Her enthusiasm is matched by the warmth of the welcome inside. Caddies full of six types of coffee bean and over 20 types of loose-leaf tea send an aroma wafting through the wood-panelled interior, with its old-fashioned counter and spiral staircase leading down to the basement. Tea is served by the pot and coffee - the beans are ground every day - comes in cafetieres. Customers can also have soups and light lunches, or sample some of the home-baked cakes and scones. The Sussex cream teas are especially popular and are a justified indulgence after hiking up Rye's hilly streets. *Mermaid Street Coffee House, 13 West Street, Rye, East Sussex TN31 7ES Tel: 01797 224858.*

Up a flight of ivy-covered steps at the foot of Rye's famous Mermaid Street, the white clapboard facade and striking blue shutters of the **Old Borough Arms** hotel make a welcome sight to any weary

**Old Borough Arms Hotel**

traveller. This very pleasant guest house offers excellent accommodations in a 300 year old former sailors' inn, incorporating part of the 14th century town wall, constructed to protect Rye from French invaders. Owners Terry and Jane Cox and their daughter Vanessa have put a bit of themselves into every part of this superb B & B. The lovely furniture is all hand-made by Terry, and it is his prized collection of vintage model cars that are on display. The breakfasts are first class, and evening meals are available on prior arrangement (local fish, when available, is a speciality). The flower bedecked patio overlooks Rye's bustling Strand, full of interesting antiques shops; the harbour is nearby. The nine ensuite rooms in this warm and cosy family run establishment fill up fast - booking is recommended. *Old Borough Arms, The Strand, Rye, East Sussex TN31 7DB Tel and Fax: 01797 222128.*

On turning right at the top of Mermaid Street, you come to the National Trust-owned ***Lamb House***, a handsome redbrick Georgian residence which was built by a local wine merchant, James Lamb, in 1723. The new building incorporated a number of earlier structures, including a 'deese' for drying herrings and a brewery which occupied the site of what is now the walled garden. In 1726, George I paid an impromptu visit to Lamb House after his ship was driven onto nearby Camber Sands during a storm. He ended up being snowed in for four nights, during which time Lamb's wife, Martha, gave birth to a son; the king agreed to be child's godfather and two days later he was baptised 'George'. An inscribed silver bowl given by the king as a christening present was later revealed to be silver plate.

Lamb House became the home of the American writer Henry James from 1898 until his death in 1916, and indeed many of his finest later novels were dictated to his secretary either in the Green Room or, during warmer weather, in the Garden Room. James laid out the delightful walled garden and invited many of his literary friends to the house, including H G Wells, Rudyard Kipling, G K Chesterton and Joseph Conrad. During the 1920s, Lamb House was leased to another writer, E F Benson, the author of the Mapp and Lucia books, who thinly disguised the house as 'Mallards' and the town as 'Tilling'. Today, Lamb House contains a number of Henry James' personal effects and is open to the public.

Not far from here, **The Hope Anchor** is a beautiful hotel with 14 good sized, well-appointed guest rooms as well as two cosy bars, guests' lounge and a handsome restaurant. Dating back to the 1750s, this lovely timbered house with its nooks, crannies and secret passages evokes a bygone age, and features in the children's books written by Malcolm Saville. It is situated in one of Rye's most enchanting and interesting cobbled streets, right in the heart of the town's wonderful conservation area, where no through traffic is allowed. Nearby landmarks include Mermaid Street, Church Square, St Mary's Church, Lamb House and the 13th century Ypres Tower within a few minutes' walk. The hotel is set in what must be Rye's highest point, affording superb views over Rye Harbour, Romney

**The Hope Anchor Hotel**

Marsh, Camber Castle and the rivers Brede and Rother. Peter and Bernadette Caldwell are the delightful hosts; their efficient, well trained staff offer guests the highest standard of accommodation and service. The restaurant's award-winning chef uses fresh, seasonally available local ingredients whenever possible to create the distinguished menu. *The Hope Anchor, Watch Bell Street, Rye, East Sussex TN31 7HA Tel: 01797 222216 Fax: 01797 223796* .

From Lamb House, it is only a very short walk to **Church Square**, Rye's wonderful centrepiece which contains some of the town's finest late-mediaeval buildings. The parish church of St Mary's was severely damaged during the French raid of 1377, although not before its church bells were taken down and carried off to Normandy. However, a retaliatory raid the following year not only inflicted a similar fate on two French towns, but succeeded in recapturing the bells of St Mary. The church was sympathetically restored during the Victorian era and contains some fine features, including a 16th century turret clock with a spectacular 18 foot pendulum, some interesting 20th century stained-glass windows, and the original 'quarter boys', 18th century cherubs which once stood above the clock face, but which have now been replaced by fibreglass replicas; these golden reproductions still come out to strike on the quarter hour (but not on the hour).

The **Town Hall** was built in 1743 and contains among its many treasures a gibbet cage holding the skull of John Breads the butcher. Fined by Mayor James Lamb in 1737 for selling short weight, Breads hatched a plan to murder Lamb, but mistakenly killed Lamb's brother in law Allen Grebell instead. The full story of this and the rest of the history of this historic town is told at the Rye Sound and Light Show.

Just a few minutes walk from the centre of Rye, nestling under the cliff and overlooking the River Rother, **The Old Vicarage** is a lovely brick-built Victorian gabled home. With its handsome balcony over the front door and trailing plants adorning the exterior, this distinctive house is full of character. The Victorian and antique furnishings hark back to the genteel pace and ambience of times past. The comfortable bedrooms, with Victorian sash windows, oil paintings and ornaments contribute to the soothing atmosphere. Owners Jonathan and Wanda Bosher have taken care to ensure their guests' every comfort. Breakfasts are served in the elegant dining room with its double aspect windows, silver, paintings, linens and lace. With fresh local produce, including award-winning local sausages, breakfast is a meal to remember. During the winter

**The Old Vicarage**

a crackling log fire adds to the guests' pleasure. Monica Edwards, the well-known children's author, lived here once; one can imagine her planning her tales of intrigue and adventure in 'Westling Harbour' (Rye Harbour). There are excellent walks to be had across marshes, down to the sea or through the nearby nature reserve. Two local pubs provide good home-cooked food. This delightful establishment offers a perfect base for exploring the ancient towns of Rye, Hastings, Canterbury and Dover and is within easy reach of many historic houses and gardens. *The Old Vicarage, Rye Harbour, East Sussex TN31 7TT Tel: 01797 222088.*

A little to the southwest is the **Ypres Tower and Museum**; one of the oldest surviving buildings in Rye, it was constructed around 1250 as a defensive fort. Two centuries later, it was acquired by John de Ypres as a private residence, then subsequently it became the town's courthouse, gaol and mortuary. Today, it houses the award-winning Rye Museum and offers some magnificent views over the surrounding coastal plain.

**The Windmill Guest House** is a Rye landmark. A working windmill up until 1910, this handsome establishment overlooking a bend in the River Tillingham offers a charming blend of old and new tasteful and modern rooms set in the context of the beautiful and impressive whitewashed clapboard mill. This unique place to stay the accommodation comprises eight double rooms and two singles

**The Windmill Guest House**

all with excellent views - stands out in more ways than one. On a site near Rye Quay and handy not just for the town centre and all amenities, but also for trips out and about in the scenic and historic East Sussex countryside - nearby attractions include Battle Abbey, site of the 1066 Norman Conquest, 600 year old Bodiam Castle, the beaches at Camber and the coast road to Hastings and other seaside towns - this attractive guest house offers real value for money.

Owners Barbara and Owen Piper are charming, gregarious hosts who go out of their way to make every visitor feel at home - the welcoming visitors' bar adds to the relaxed and friendly ambience in this fine establishment. *The Windmill Guest House, Mill Lane, Off Ferry Road, Rye, East Sussex TN31 7DW Tel: 01797 224027.*

The nearly 1,800 acre **Rye Harbour Nature Reserve** spans much of the large tract of land bounded by the River Rother, the sea and the Royal Military Canal. A Site of Special Scientific Interest, the reserve has some of the finest coastal shingle vegetation anywhere in England.

# Around Rye

### *Playden*                                                          *Map 4 ref S5*
*1 mile N of Rye off the A268*

The hamlet of Playden has a 12th century church (**St Michael's**) with a shingled broach spire. Inside, there is an unusual memorial to a 16th century Flemish brewer which is engraved with a pair of beer barrels; these would originally have been inlaid with brass. The settlement also contains a couple of elegant country residences: **Leasam House**, which was constructed of red brick in the 1800s, and ***The Cherries***, which contains an interesting private museum of rural history.

The country lanes to the northeast of Playden lead to the start of the ***Royal Military Canal***, an unusual inland waterway which was built in 1804 as part of the nation's defences against Napoleon. The 20 mile towpath between Rye and Hythe offers some easy and attractive walking along the northern fringe of the now-drained Walland and Romney Marshes. There are some pleasant picnic spots along the length of the canal, a section of which is now owned by the National Trust.

## Peasmarsh
*Map 4 ref S4*

*3 miles NW of Rye off the A268*

Here in the village of Peasmarsh, ***The Church of St Peter and St Paul*** is worth a visit. Still largely Norman, with a battlement tower and a broach spire, it retains a superb Norman chancel arch, decorated with carvings of heraldic animals. Four of the church bells were cast in 1631, making them far older than most still in use.

## Winchelsea
*Map 4 ref S6*

*2 miles SW of Rye off the A259*

The journey from Rye to Winchelsea passes the ruins of ***Camber Castle***, a fortification built in 1539 by Henry VIII as part of the Tudor coastal defences. Although originally constructed near the shoreline, the shifting sands have marooned the structure over a mile inland.

The ancient Cinque Port of Winchelsea is the smallest town in England and one of the earliest to be subjected to the machinations of the town planner. Until the 13th century, Winchelsea lay several miles to the south on a site which was eventually engulfed by the sea following a series of violent storms. In its place, a new town was laid out its present position on Iham Hill which was designed to a rigid grid plan drawn up in part by Edward I. Built along Roman lines, the ambitious rectangular pattern of 39 squares covered a total area of 89 acres and, for two centuries, became home to some 6,000 inhabitants, around 10 times the present number.

For a short period in the early 14th century, Winchelsea was perhaps the most important of the Channel ports, carrying on a thriving wine trade and supplying 13 of the 57 ships which made up the total Cinque Port fleet. However, the unpredictable forces of nature caused the sea to retreat once again, an occurrence which stranded Winchelsea without a port or a means of sustaining its economy. Neither the town walls nor the sizable parish church of

***St Thomas*** was ever completed (it remains a magnificent fragment, with only the side chapels and choir left), and the town gradually shrank into an area of a dozen or so blocks in the northeastern quarter of Edward's original layout. Of the town's three surviving gateways, ***Strand Gate***, is a classic example of a mediaeval drum tower gate and marks the entrance to the town via the A259. On the north side, ***Pipewell Gate*** guards the minor road across the Brede valley. The ***New Gate*** is located at the southern end of town, where bumps in the grassy fields and a few arches are all that remain of the days of the French raids.

Assisted by a gradual recovery which began in the mid 19th century, present-day Winchelsea is a place with great historic beauty. The town has its own special atmosphere which has long attracted artists and writers, including Turner, Millais, Thackeray and Conrad. Of the town's many historic buildings, ***Court Hall*** is among the oldest in the county and now contains a small, yet informative, local history museum. The ruins of a 14th century Franciscan Friary, the Grey Friars, can also be seen within the grounds of a home for the elderly in Friars Road. Further details can be obtained by studying the information board on the green, or by following the instructive walking guide published by the local council.

# CHAPTER SIX
## Ashdown Forest & The Sussex Weald

*Bewl Water*

# Chapter 6 - Area Covered

*For precise location of places please refer to the colour maps found at the rear of the book.*

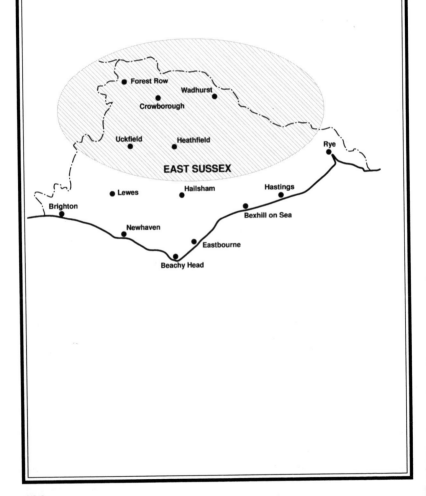

# 6
# *Ashdown Forest & The Sussex Weald*

## Introduction

Home to Rudyard Kipling, A A Milne and many significant centres of traditional crafts, history and classic English countryside, this region of East Sussex is perhaps best known for the Weald, famed for its undulating woodlands, weatherboarded and pantile-hung cottages, traditional hall-houses and unspoilt farmland dotted with fine homes such as Bateman's in Burwash, and attractive gardens such as those at Kidbrooke Park in Forest Row and Pashley Manor in Ticehurst. In centuries gone by the Weald was deeply forested, its oaks supplying the timber that built the British Navy. Trees were also felled to fuel the charcol burners used to smelt Sussex iron. Now it is more a landscape of hedge rows and pastured ridges affording marvellous views.

Along with the unique Wealden landscape, the miles of Ashdown Forest offer lovely landscapes and recreation options, from walking and angling to hang-gliding and mountain biking. The numerous picturesque villages and parishes also offer tranquil delights and scenes of bucolic splendour.

## Heathfield

Heathfield grew to become an important market town with the coming of the former Tunbridge Wells to Eastbourne railway. The parish church in Old Heathfield has a 13th century tower with a shingled spire; nearby **Heathfield Park** estate was once owned by General Sir George Augustus Elliot (later Lord Heathfield), commander of the British garrison during the Siege of Gibraltar in 1779-82. Gibraltar Tower in the grounds was erected in his honour. The main house was remodelled in the 19th century and incorporates parts of earlier 17th and 18th century structures.

Here in this tranquil town, set in three-quarters of an acre of peaceful, well-tended gardens filled with ornamental shrubs, towering trees and colourful bedding plants, *'Iwood'* is a very pleasant and well-appointed bed and breakfast establishment offering a high standard of accommodation. Set on a quiet road within walking distance of the centre of Heathfield, this large, brick-built B&B offers complete privacy and comfort. Spotlessly clean, well-furnished and

*'Iwood' Bed & Breakfast*

tastefully decorated, the facilities provided in this faultless establishment are three charming double bedrooms, one with country style sitting room and bath, one ensuite, and the third sharing bathroom with the owners. The cosy and comfortable breakfast room affords superb views of the South Downs and the English Channel, to be enjoyed as guests savour the delicious home-cooked breakfasts. Co-owner Jean Morren is a conscientious and warm hostess, keen to make all her guests most welcome. There are also some fine pubs and restaurants in the area for evening meals. No smoking. Children welcome. *'Iwood', Mutton Hall Lane, Heathfield, East Sussex TN21 8NR Tel: 01435 863918; 0468 917816.*

# Around Heathfield

## *Cross in Hand*                    *Map 3 ref N5*
*2 miles W of Heathfield off the A265*

Here in this intringuingly named community, at the large junction there is an old post mill, which at one time stood five miles to the west at Uckfield.

**The Cross in Hand Inn** is a part-timbered public house, restaurant and bed and breakfast in the village that gives the pub its name, some two miles west of Heathfield, just off the A267. Dating back in parts to the 15th century - as the exposed oak beams and

*The Cross in Hand*

wood panelling attest - this welcoming establishment has been renovated with great care and attention by Mo and Jackie Chatfield, the friendly and conscientious proprietors. The fine selection of real ales can be enjoyed in front of the crackling log fires in winter, or in the peaceful beer garden in summer. The two B&B rooms are cosy and comfortable, with exposed beams and sloping floors. Breakfast is available for residents and non-residents alike, as well as a good choice of tasty lunches, bar snacks and evening meals, seven days a week; the sumptuous traditional Sunday lunch - a local legend. Ensure a table by booking in advance. For traditional home comforts and real value for money, The Cross in Hand is hard to beat. *The Cross in Hand Inn, Cross in Hand, Heathfield, East Sussex Tel: 01435 862053.*

## Waldron
*Map 3 ref N5*

*3 miles SE of Heathfield off the A267*

The **Church of All Saints** in Waldron is approached through a lych-gate, shingled with thick Horsham slate tiles. Unusual for its 13th century provenance, it has very wide aisle and nave. There is also a lovely kingpost roof.

## Burwash
*Map 4 ref P4*

*5 miles E of Heathfield off the A265*

This exceptionally pretty village has a High Street lined with delightful, predominantly 17th and 18th century timber-framed and weather-boarded houses and shops, many of them now converted to handsome bed and breakfast establishments. The village sign testifies to the fact that this was once an important centre of the Wealden iron industry.

The beautiful whitewashed brick and pan-tiled roof contribute to the seafront feel of **Villiers**, a delightful bed and breakfast establishment here on the High Street in Burwash. The accommodations in this 17th century Grade II listed cottage - part of a larger house now subdivided into three separate cottages - have been completely restored and redecorated within the last two years, and comprise one double-bedroom with ensuite sitting room and private bath, and a twin-bedded attic room and shared bath. Both rooms afford superb views over the Rother valley to the north. There is excellent walking in the area, and visitors are welcome to make use of the lovely gardens and terrace. Mrs Sue Jennings, the hospitable proprietor, takes the time and care to make every guest's visit memorable - including providing picnic

*Villiers*

lunches if requested in advance (just the thing for an outing to Glyndebourne, only 30 minutes away), and having on hand the latest catalogues for nearby specialist garden nurseries - Merriments,

Washfield and High Banks, Axletree and Perryhill. *Villiers, High Street, Burwash, East Sussex TN19 7ET Tel: 01435 882624.*

Among the exceptional buildings in Burwash High Street is **Rampyndene**, a handsome timber-framed house with a sweeping roof which was built in 1699 by a wealthy local timber merchant.

The parish church of **St Bartholomew** has a broach spire and a Norman tower dated 1090. Set into the wall at the end of the south aisle is a 14th century iron slab marking the grave of a local iron-founder which is believed to be the earliest example of its kind in the country. Near the door of the church there is a bronze plaque commemorating Rudyard Kipling's only son, John, who was killed at Loos during the First World War.

**Church House** is a handsome Georgian village house offering bed and breakfast, with a beautiful porticoed facade, set back from the road by a low brick wall and attractive front garden. Overlooking the parish church of St Bartholomew, this welcoming, intimate B&B maintains an air of peace and tranquillity. Exquisitely decorated and furnished - the bedding is luxurious, the furnishings su-

**Church House**

premely comfortable - this is first and foremost a family home, and owner Rosemary Sendall is keen to make every guest feel a part of it. The period detail and nicely proportioned rooms speak of more gracious times past. Outside, the lovely gardens offer a haven of tranquillity. There is also superb birdwatching or walking from this picturesque starting point, and guests will find Church House a wonderful base from which to explore this part of Sussex and down to Eastbourne, Hastings, and other points on the coast. Early booking is recommended. *Church House, High Street, Burwash, Nr Etchingham, East Sussex TN19 7EH Tel: 01435 883282.*

Rudyard Kipling moved to Burwash from Rottingdean in 1902, it is said to combat the growing problem of overenthusiastic sightseers, and lived here until his death in 1936. The superb Jacobean house which became his home is located down a steep and narrow

**Bateman's**

lane which runs south from the A265 to the west of the village centre. **Bateman's** was originally constructed for a prosperous local iron-master in 1634 and is set within 33 acres of beautiful grounds which were landscaped by Kipling himself.

Now under the ownership of the National Trust, the house amounts to a fascinating museum of the author's life. The interior is furnished with his portraits, private effects and possessions, and his study remains exactly as it was at the time of his death. Kipling's 1928 Rolls Royce stills sits in the garage, and there is a working water mill in the grounds which he used for grinding corn. One of the oldest working water-driven turbines in the country can be seen nearby; this was originally installed by Kipling to provide power to the house. Please phone for opening details and admission costs (tel: 01435 882302).

One of Kipling's most famous works, *Puck of Pook's Hill*, was written at Bateman's and is said to refer to the wooded hilltop which can be seen from his study window. This area to the southwest of the house provides some particularly fine walking through the valley of the River Dudwell and up onto Pook's Hill. Access can be gained from the grounds of Bateman's or from the lane which runs between Burwash Weald and Brightling.

Another option for those wishing to stay for a longer visit in this area of East Sussex, the ***Burwash Motel*** offers a night to remember with its handsome Tudor-style decor, four-poster beds and magnificent views overlooking the Dudwell Valley. Standing adjacent to Bateman's, former home of Rudyard Kipling, the immediate neighbourhood also has associations with 'Puck of Pook Hill'; the site of the Battle of Hastings is only a short drive away. The village has a

**Burwash Motel**

entle, peaceful atmosphere that is essentially Sussex. The adjoing Bear Inn is one of Burwash's oldest places of rest and refreshent, which has since the 17th century offered the pilgrim, traveler or tourist welcoming hospitality. The Main Bar has a cosy atosphere and an inglenook log fire; here bar meals and fine ales an be enjoyed. The Kipling restaurant offers a wide selection of ome-made dishes; guests are welcome to book for the Sunday roast erved from the carvery. The Bear Inn also has a pleasant and quiet beer garden with views over the beautiful Sussex countryside; whilst relaxing over a pint of real ale, you may wish to try a game of boules. *Burwash Motel & Bear Inn, High Street, Burwash, East Sussex TN19 7ET Tel: 01435 882540; 01435 882260.*

## Brightling

*Map 4 ref P5*

*6 miles E of Heathfield off the B2096*

The extraordinary village of Brightling is perhaps best known for one of its former residents, the Georgian eccentric, 'Mad' Jack Fuller, who was not only a local ironmaster and squire, but was also a generous philanthropist and the long serving MP for East Sussex. He was also one of the first people to recognise the talent of the artist J M W Turner, and was responsible for saving Bodiam Castle from complete destruction. (He also weighed some 22 stone and was affectionately referred to as the 'Hippopotamus'.)

Perhaps Fuller's most visible legacy is the series of imaginative follies which he commissioned to provide employment for his workers during the decline of the local iron industry. Among these is the **Brightling Observatory**, now a private house, the **Rotunda Temple** in Brightling Park, and the **Brightling Needle**, a 40 foot stone obelisk which was erected on a rise to the north of the village which at 650 feet above sea level, is the second highest point in East Sussex. Another of Fuller's follies was built as a result of a wager. After having laid a bet on the number of church spires which were visible from Brightling Park, he returned home to discover that one he had taken into account, Dallington, could not in fact be seen. He solved the problem by getting a party of workmen to hastily erect a 35 foot mock spire in a meadow near Woods Corner which is now referred to as the **Sugar Loaf**.

The parish church of **St Thomas a Becket** contains an impressive Gothic style barrel organ which Fuller presented to the parish in 1820. Ten years earlier, and 24 years before his death, Fuller erected a personal mausoleum in the churchyard in the shape of a 25 foot pyramid.

## Herstmonceux

*Map 4 ref O*

*6 miles SE of Heathfield off the A271*

Herstmonceux (pronounced Herst-mon-soo) is of course famous for **Herstmonceux Castle and Observatory**. Built on the site of an earlier Norman manor house in 1440 by Sir Roger Fiennes, the castle was one of the first large-scale buildings in Britain to be constructed from redbrick; it was also one of the first fortifications

**Herstmonceux Castle**

take into account both the defensive needs and the comfort of its residents.

Later, the castle passed into the hands of the Hare family, who presided over a long period of decline which culminated in its virtual dismantling in 1777. The structure then remained in a state of dilapidation for some 150 years until a major programme of restoration began in the 1930s under the supervision of the Lewes architect, W H Godfrey. His careful and inspired work helped to restore the turrets and battlements to their former glory and today, the fully refurbished castle stands in pristine condition at the centre of its highly photogenic moat.

In 1948, the Royal Greenwich Observatory moved here from its original home in Greenwich Park, London to get away from the residual glare of the city. Over the following 20 years, the mighty **Isaac Newton telescope** was planned and built in the grounds which, when it was officially opened in 1967, was one of the five largest telescopes in the world.

Recent advances in the field of astronomy necessitated a further move, and the Royal Greenwich Observatory is now located in Cambridge. The premises are now used for an International Studies Centre.

Flower filled baskets line the exterior of **The Brewer's Arms**, an attractive main road pub here in the village of Herstmonceux.

**The Brewer's Arms**

This lovely whitewashed clapboard building has been on this site since 1580 and has been in its day a tanner's and, until the early 1800s, a butcher's shop; after standing empty for some months it was resurrected three years ago by proprietors Barb and Barry Dimmack. Their hard work and experience in the pub trade have resulted in a fine, family run - and very popular - establishment. They serve real ales (including Broadside, Butcombe, Red Macgregor, Harveys and Red Fox) and a choice from a varied menu: burritos, Jamaican chicken and lamb noisettes, as well as vegetarian options, but also hearty English staples such as fish platters (smoked salmon, smoked mackerel, prawns and mussels) with salad and granary bread, and rhubarb tart and custard for pudding. Winner of a Good Beer Guide award, the interior has masses of exposed beams and fine country cottage furnishings. The garden is relaxing and peaceful, with a boules pit. *Brewer's Arms, Gardner Street, Herstmonceux, East Sussex BN27 4LB Tel: 01323 832226.*

Opposite the entrance to Herstmonceux Castle stands **All Saints Church**, a handsome building dating from 1180 which was built on the site of an earlier Saxon structure. Inside, there is an unusual rectangular font which was carved from Wealden sandstone around 1380 and a number of exceptional memorials.

A centre for craft industries for centuries, Herstmonceux is particularly famous for its traditional woodworking and, in particular for the making of 'trugs', handmade wooden gardeners' baskets which are made from broad bands of willow on an ash or chestnut frame which originated during the time of the Great Exhibition of 1851.

The traditional willow and chestnut baskets, or trugs, crafted and sold at **The Truggery** are ideal for a wide variety of uses. Deriving from the Anglo-Saxon word 'trog', meaning a wooden vessel or boat-shaped article, trugs are renowned for their strength, durability and beauty.

**The Truggery**

At this, one of the few remaining trug-makers in the country, where three generations of trug makers have worked, customers are invited to see Sussex trugs being made in the traditional way by local craftsmen, as they have been for over 200 years. The handle and rim are of sweet chestnut, the boards of cricket bat willow. Chestnut trees were first planted in Britain by the Romans and grow in abundance, so there is no danger of depleting the source. The trugs come in a variety of lovely shapes and sizes, and custom made hand-painted trugs can also be commissioned. For a beautiful and practical tool and a wonderful souvenir of Sussex, do visit. The shop is open 10 a.m. to 5 p.m. Tuesday to Saturday, and some Sundays and Bank Holidays (ring ahead). Mail order service also available. *The Truggery, Coopers Croft, Herstmonceux, Hailsham, East Sussex BN27 1QL Tel/Fax: 01323 832314.*

### Dallington
*Map 4 ref O5*
*4 miles E of Heathfield off the B2096*
Dallington's **Church of St Giles** possesses one of only a handful of stone built spires in Sussex and is adjoined by an attractive timber-framed house.

### Buxted                                              Map 3 ref M4
*5 miles W of Heathfield on the A272*
Buxted village was rebuilt in its present position in the early 19th
century when Lord Liverpool, the owner of nearby **Buxted Park**,
wanted to clear his estate of unsightly domestic dwellings. The much
restored 13th century church of St Margaret remained within the
grounds; it features an 18th century shingled broach spire and a
Jacobean pulpit which was used by William Wordsworth's brother
when he was vicar here. Lord Liverpool's Georgian country mansion, Buxted House, was almost destroyed by fire in 1940.

### Hadlow Down                                         Map 3 ref N4
*3 miles E of Buxted off the A272*
Undulating lanes wind their way through some of loveliest countryside in the Weald and eventually lead to this handsome hamlet.
Just outside Hadlow Down is **Wilderness Wood**, 60 acres of working woodland which are run as a living museum of woodland man-
agement, where wood has been grown for almost 1,000 years. The
barn, built using genuine medieval techniques of wattle and daub,
houses a detailed display about the growth and use of wood. The
woodland trail changes seasonally.

### Piltdown                                            Map 3 ref L5
*5 miles W of Buxted off the A272*
The narrow lanes to the northwest of Beeches Farm lead to the
village of Piltdown, a place notorious in academic circles for being
the site of one the greatest archeological hoaxes of all time. In 1912,
an ancient skull was discovered by the amateur archeologist, Charles
Dawson, which was believed to form the missing link between man
and the apes. The Piltdown Skull was believed to be about 150,000
years old; however, improved methods of dating in 1949 showed that
the jaw bone in fact belonged to a young orang-utan, whilst the rest
was a human skull dating from mediaeval times. The perpetrator of
the hoax was never discovered; however, various theories point the
finger at Sir Arthur Conan Doyle, at an evangelical Christian fun-
damentalist, or perhaps most likely, at Charles Dawson himself.

### Maresfield                                          Map 3 ref L4
*4 miles NW of Buxted off the A22*
Maresfield is a sizable village which, thankfully, is now bypassed by
the main A22 London to Eastbourne road. This was a remote spot
before the road builders finally managed to conquer the dense forest of the Weald in the 18th century. With the coming of the new

roads, however, Maresfield's position at the junction of two through routes helped it grow into an important staging point, and the Georgian Chequers Inn, perhaps the oldest building in Maresfield, is a fine example of a former coaching inn which survives from this period. St Bartholomew's Church is Norman in parts; there is a Norman window in the nave. The western side of the building is mediaeval. There is a lovely rose window in the north transept.

## Fairwarp
*Map 3 ref M4*

*4 miles NW of Buxted off the A26*

This small village on the southern slopes of Ashdown Forest is mentioned as far back as 1519, as Fayre Wharpe. Its Christ Church is a handsome Victorian sandstone structure designed by Rhode Hawkins. During the 1930s, Sir Bernard Eckstein, whose father had lived at nearby Oldlands Hall, added the tower and chancel and the Italian marble flooring. In the churchyard there are three impressive memorials to the Eckstein family designed by the artist Sir William Reid Dick.

*Broom Cottage* is an impressive and charming white-washed brick cottage built in 1874, offering bed and breakfast accommodation. Situated down a very quiet country lane in the heart of Ashdown Forest, the guest bedrooms in this distinguished establishment are decorated and furnished to the highest standards of taste. Owner Jane Rattray used to run an antiques business, and has made use of the benefit of her experience and expertise to make this superb B&B the last word in cottage-style comfort. The truly delightful and rest-

*Broom Cottage*

ful ambience will satisfy the most discerning visitor. Jane's lovely paintings adorn the walls; some of her other intricate and colourful paintings are available to buy. The attractive and extensive gardens are a haven of peace and relaxation, the breakfasts a delight, and there is an excellent local pub for evening meals just 15 minutes' walk away. This comfortable and homely B&B is extremely popular and very reasonably priced, so do book in advance. *Broom Cottage, Browns Brook, Fairwarp, East Sussex TN22 3BY Tel: 01825 712942.*

## Ticehurst
*Map 4 ref P3*

*9 miles NE of Heathfield on the B2099*

Ticehurst is an ancient village filled with the attractive tile-hung and white weather-boarded buildings which are so characteristic of the settlements along the Kent-Sussex border. There are a number of noteworthy buildings here, including **Furze House**, a former workhouse, and **Whatman's**, an old carpenter's cottage with strangely curving exterior walls. The parish church of St Mary dates primarily from the 13th and 14th centuries, though it was restored in 1879. It contains a stained-glass window depicting scenes from the Last Judgment which is made up of fragments of mediaeval glass. The 16th century font cover is exceptionally fine.

**Bewl Water**

In 1975, the Southern Water Authority dammed the valley of the River Bewl to the north of Ticehurst to create **Bewl Bridge Reservoir**, the largest area of inland water in southeast England. A great many buildings were drowned in the process; however, one, the 15th century **Dunsters Mill**, was taken down brick by brick and moved to its present location above the new high water level. (A couple of timber-framed farm buildings found their way to the Weald and Downland Museum at Singleton in West Sussex.) The reservoir now offers a great many attractions for the visitor, including walking, picnicking, trout fishing and pleasure boat trips.

**Pashley Manor Gardens** feature fine beds across the south front, a wide lawn and a moat leading to the manor itself. Numerous varieties of shrub roses, paeonies, hydrangea and many other plants bring fantastic colour and lushness to every corner. The 'Golden Garden' leads down to woodlands and a chain of ponds surrounded by rhododendrons, azaleas and climbing roses reflected in the still, dark waters.

## Etchingham
*Map 4 ref P4*
*2 miles S of Ticehurst off the A265*

The scattered settlement of Etchingham is set in the broad lush valley of the River Rother. The village possesses the Decorated **Church of the Assumption of St Nicholas**, said to be the finest 14th century church in Sussex. It contains some fine monumental brasses to the de Echyngham family. **Haremere Hall**, to the southeast of the railway station, is an impressive 17th century manor open to the public as a shire-horse centre.

## Wadhurst
*Map 4 ref P3*
*4 miles NW of Ticehurst off the B2099*

The village of Wadhurst was another great centre of the Wealden iron industry in the 17th and 18th centuries, and one of the last places in Sussex to hold out against the improved coal-fired smelting techniques which had taken root in the North. The floor of the parish church of **St Peter and St Paul** is inlaid with a unique collection of around 30 iron tomb slabs which mark the graves of local iron-masters who died between 1617 and 1772. Many are inscribed with curiously worded messages or elaborate heraldic designs, and resonate strangely to the sound of visitors' footsteps.

Several of Wadhurst's find old buildings date from the heyday of the local iron industry. These include the timber-framed Church Gate House near the churchyard, the Queen Anne vicarage in the High Street, and the tile-hung Hill House next door. At Cousley Wood, two miles northeast of the village, is a very pretty 18th century manor called **Ladyheads**.

Three miles to the west of Wadhurst, **Nap Wood** offers some exceptional walking through 107 acres of National Trust-owned oak woodland. The area is maintained as a nature reserve by the Sussex Wildlife Trust and can be found on the eastern side of the A267 between Mark Cross and Frant.

## Frant
*Map 3 ref N2*
*6 miles NW of Ticehurst off the A267*

Frant is another former iron-founding community which contains an early 19th century church with some unusual interior features, and a country house, **Shernfold Park**, which was once the home of the founder of Ottawa in Canada. St Alban's Church was built in 1821 in Perpendicular style. The village's charming Victorian railway station is one mile away at Bells Yew Green, a small and picturesque hamlet.

## Bayham Abbey
*Map 4 ref O2*
*5 miles NW of Ticehurst off the B2169*

Bayham Abbey is a ruined early 13th century monastery which lies on the Kent-Sussex boundary, in the valley of the River Teise, a tributary of the Medway which is famous for its trout. Despite falling into disrepair following the Dissolution of the Monasteries, much of this once powerful and influential monastic house remains.

**Bartley Mill**, a restored 13th century water mill, originally belonged to the estate of Bayham Abbey and is now part of a 180 acre organic farm which supplies cereals and other produce to shops and bakeries throughout the locality. Part of the output is ground into flour on the premises, and this and number of other home-produced foods, such as muesli, bread and cakes, are available in the farm shop and tearooms. The grounds also contain a farm trail, picnic area, trout hatchery and falconry centre.

## Mayfield
*Map 3 ref N4*
*4 miles SW of Ticehurst off the A267*

Mayfield is an ancient settlement which possesses one of the finest main streets in East Sussex. According to local legend, St Dunstan, a skilled blacksmith by trade, paused here in the 10th century to deliver the people of this remote Wealden community from the clutches of paganism. On this occasion, however, he was confronted by the Devil himself who, disguised as a beautiful woman, attempted to seduce the missionary as he worked at his anvil. However, Dunstan spotted that the feet of his young temptress were in fact cloven and, recognising her as Satan, grabbed her by the nose with a pair of red hot tongs. The Devil gave out an almighty scream and beat a hasty retreat; however, he returned soon after, this time disguised as a traveller in need of new shoes for his horse. Dunstan again saw through the deception and, threatening Satan with his blacksmith's tools, forced him to promise never again to enter a house which had a horseshoe above its door.

St Dunstan went on to become the Archbishop of Canterbury in 959 and, some time later, an Archbishops' palace was built in Mayfield, the remains of which include a large mediaeval hall whose roof is supported by a series of colossal stone arches. The site is now occupied by **The Catholic Convent of the Holy Child**, a convent school which is approached through a 15th century gatehouse in the High Street. Yeomans, a partially remodelled 15th century hall-house stands almost opposite the gatehouse, and a little further along, the Middle House has been converted from an imposing oak-beamed Tudor residence into one of the finest country inns in Sussex.

St Dunstan built a simple timber church in Mayfield which was replaced by a stone structure in the 13th century; this had to rebuilt after a fire destroyed much of the village in 1389 and again after the building was damaged by lightning in 1621. The present-day **St Dunstan's** contains a Jacobean pulpit, a font dated 1666 and some impressive 17th and 18th century monuments to the Baker family. **Argos Hill** to the northwest of the village offers some magnificent views over the surrounding landscape. It is also the location of an old post mill which now houses an interesting local museum; opening times displayed on site.

### Mark Cross                                    *Map 3 ref N3*
*5 miles W of Ticehurst off the B2100*

**Houndsell Cottage** is located in quiet countryside between Wadhurst and the village of Mark Cross. It is surrounded by forest and set in four acres of tranquil surrounding fields, and provides comfortable bed and breakfast accommodation. This 1920s converted farmworker's cottage has leaded windows and, inside, a massive York stone fireplace in the lounge. The large breakfast room runs the length of the house and overlooks extensive, mature gardens which are well kept and afford a lovely view. The guest rooms (one twin/triple on the ground floor, one twin and two singles upstairs) are furnished with oak chests of drawers and wardrobes. The bathroom is large and luxurious, and offers a country view from the wide windows. Owners Brian and Shirley Sears have created the perfect retreat: cosy, quiet and relaxed. Brian is a keen photographer and samples of his work, depicting their travels around the

**Houndsell Cottage**

world, adorn every room. Houndsell Cottage makes an excellent base for touring Sussex and Kent, visiting the many castles, gardens and stately homes. *Houndsell Cottage, Mark Cross, Crowborough, East Sussex TN6 3PF Tel: 01892 782292.*

## Crowborough

The scattered community of Crowborough, at over 750 feet above sea level, is one of the highest towns in Sussex. Some splendid views over the High Weald can be enjoyed from the summit of Crowborough Beacon near the centre of town. Before the arrival of the railway in the 1860s, all that existed here was a lonely settlement populated by iron-smelters and brigands. However, the new rail link soon attracted commuters keen to escape the grime of Victorian London and gradually transformed Crowborough into a flourishing residential town. Its convenient location also attracted a number of well-known writers around this time, in particular Arthur Conan Doyle, the author of the Sherlock Holmes stories.

Recent residential and retail developments have made Crowborough into a prosperous modern town with good shopping and recreational facilities.

***Madhatters*** is an attractive bed and breakfast on Green Lane in Crowborough, not far from the town centre off the B2157. This warm and welcoming bungalow has two guest rooms available; both are decorated to a high standard of comfort. The handsome rear garden is tastefully planted with shrubs, trees and a variety of flowers, and makes a restful place to relax. Centrally situated for touring in the area, this charming establishment is run with care by amiable and gregarious owner Yvonne Franks, who is conscientious about ensuring her guests' comfort and privacy. Guests are welcome to come and go as they please, and so feel immediately at ease in

**Madhatters**

these pleasant surroundings. With plenty of good restaurants and pubs nearby, and Ashdown Forest close at hand, Madhatters makes an excellent base from which to explore all this region has to offer. *Madhatters, Green Lane, Crowborough, East Sussex TN6 2BX Tel: 01892 654921.*

## Ashdown Forest

*Map 3 ref L3*

*2 miles W of Crowborough off the B2188*

This, the largest area of land in the southeast of England which has never been under the plough, is an extensive region of open heath and woodland on the high ridges of the Weald.

The original meaning of the word 'forest' was 'Royal Hunting Area', and this is precisely what Ashdown Forest used to be. The earliest records (dating from 1268) indicate that the region's thriving population of deer made it a popular hunting ground for royalty and noblemen. Before the end of the 13th century, the forest was enclosed by a 'pale' - a ditch and bank topped by a wooden fence making it difficult for the deer to jump over. Keen royal huntsmen such as Henry VIII and James I visited Ashdown fairly often.

In the chaos that was the English Civil War, the forest was neglected and, by 1657, no deer at all remained there. After many wrangles at the hands of competing would-be developers, the area was divided roughly into two: one went to speculator Alexander Staples, the other preserved for the people, to use for grazing and woodcutting.

In the 18th and 19th centuries many more claims were made on the land and resources, culminating in 1885 in an Act of Parliament affording public rights of access to specified areas of the forest for recreational purposes. In 1974, a new Act allowed public access (on foot) to wander the whole of the forest.

There are many picnic areas and scenic viewpoints, a few public footpaths and, once again, deer, which can be seen in the more remote areas. Further information on what to do and see in the forest can be found at the Ashdown Forest Centre, one mile east of Wych Cross on the Coleman's Hatch road.

### Groombridge
*Map 3 ref N2*

*3 miles NE of Crowborough off the B2110*

The charming, unspoilt village of Groombridge stands on the Sussex-Kent border. At the centre of the village there is a triangular green which is surrounded by a group of attractive 15th and 16th century estate cottages, a handsome 17th century **Dower House** and a church which began life as the chapel of nearby **Groombridge Place**. This impressive moated redbrick country mansion lies a short distance away across open parkland and was built to a characteristic 'H' design in the mid-17th century on the site of an earlier structure. It is set within beautiful terraced gardens (open certain days) known as the Enchanted Forest, which is believed to have been planned by John Evelyn, the 17th century English diarist.

### Withyham
*Map 3 ref M2*

*3 miles NW of Crowborough off the B2110*

Withyham is a pleasant community which is loosely arranged around an attractive green. The village church of **St Michael and All Angels**, high on a hill outside the village, was built in the mid-17th century to replace an earlier structure which burnt down after having been struck by lightning. Inside, there is an impressive mural of the Last Judgement painted by the Earl de la Warr, the rector here in the mid-19th century. The surrounding area, and indeed much of Ashdown Forest, was once owned by the Earls' family, the Sackvilles, several of whom are buried in the Sackville Chapel. This section of the church contains an exceptional group of carved stone monuments, including an inscribed slate memorial to Vita Sackville-West, the poet and co-owner of Sissinghurst Garden in Kent who died in

1962, as well as an unusual collection of 18th century flags belonging to the Dukes of Dorset.

**The Dorset Arms** public house takes its name and insignia from the arms of the Sackville family, once Earls of Dorset, whose seat is at the nearby Buckhurst Park. Dating back to the mid-1400s, this former farmhouse building retains many fascinating original features - the wall and beamed ceiling in the restaurant are Elizabethan, and part of the kitchen is built into an ice-cave deep in the hillside behind the pub. The floor in the bar is fashioned from Sussex oak, and the magnificent log fires and collection of horse brasses

*The Dorset Arms*

and wall plates on display all add to the cosy ambience of this traditional country pub. The Dorset Arms enjoys and excellent reputation for good home-cooked food, all of it fresh. The lunch and dinner menus offer a range of tempting options; the real ales are locally produced by Harveys of Lewes. *The Dorset Arms, Withyam, East Sussex TN7 4BD Tel: 01892 770278.*

## *Hartfield*                                   *Map 3 ref M2*
*4 miles NW of Crowborough off the B2110*

Hartfield, an old hunting settlement which takes its name from the adult male red deer, or hart. The 13th century village church of St Mary's has a tower with a shingled broach spire and an unusual roofed churchyard gate. Close by stands an early 16th century timber-framed cottage with an overhanging upper storey which, appropriately, is known as the Lychgate.

A A Milne, author of the much loved Winnie the Pooh stories, lived at Cotchford Farm, half a mile south of Hartfield. Along with the artist E H Shepard, he made the landscape of Ashdown Forest come alive to millions of young readers throughout the world. The timber bridge spanning the small tributary of the Medway where Milne's son, Christopher Robin, would meet with his fictitious friends to play 'Poohsticks', was restored in 1979 by Milne's publishers and East Sussex County Council.

If you are a fan of Winnie the Pooh, you will want to visit 'Pooh Corner' while in Hartfield. You will certainly find your tastes catered for, as this shop is full of *'Pooh-phanalia'*. The building was built at around 1690 and has low ceilings - so mind your head.

## Forest Row                                             Map 3 ref L2
*6 miles NW of Crowborough off the A22*

Forest Row is a hillside village in Ashdown Forest, on the A22 London to Eastbourne road. It is popular with walkers and also a good starting point for wonderful forest drives.

This pioneering 'waste-edge' settlement was founded in the late Middle Ages as a single row of cottages on the fringe of Ashdown Forest. At that time the forest was part of the dense and, in places, impenetrable swathe of vegetation which covered the Weald and effectively separated the Thames Valley from the south coast. The Romans knew the forest as *Silva Anderida* and were the first to cut a way through to connect the city of Londinium with their fortified settlement on the south coast at Pevensey.

The impressive *Brambletye Hotel* is located here in picturesque Forest Row. Once a private residence, it has been an hotel since 1866, numbering among its famed guests of the past one Arthur Conan Doyle. This elegant establishment offers a choice of eateries: the Deerstalker Restaurant, an excellent carvery with an extensive range of seafood, steak, chicken, duck, pork and vegetarian dishes, to be followed by home-made desserts; and Black Peter's bar, a cosy nook with exposed beams where you can partake of tasty sandwiches, pies, grilled meals or vegetarian alternative. And to drink? Real ales on tap, including locally-brewed Harveys of Lewes best bitter. The ambience throughout is brimming with old-world charm. Hospitable owner Edward Booth and his very friendly staff are anxious to make every guest's visit special - there is a spacious patio for lounging in summer, a large selection of books in the lovely reception area, and even an antique writing desk in the bar anteroom - one of the many features in this fine hotel that harken back to more

**Brambletye Hotel**

gracious days. *The Brambletye Hotel, The Square, Forest Row, East Sussex RH18 5EZ Tel: 01342 824144 Fax: 01342 824833.*

Forest Row not only provides an excellent base for exploring the area; it is also surrounded by a number of interesting country houses, including **Kidbrooke Park**, three quarters of a mile to the south-west, which dates from the early 18th century and has a garden designed by Repton. Ashdown House, one mile to the northeast, was designed in the 1790s by the architect responsible for several fine buildings in Baltimore and Philadelphia.

## Wych Cross                                    *Map 3 ref L3*
*6 miles W of Crowborough off the A22*

Wych Cross marks the western limit of Ashdown. Local folklore has it that its name derives from a cross erected at the spot where the body of Richard de Wyche, Bishop of Chichester (c 1197-1253), was rested overnight on the journey from Kent to Chichester for burial.

*Wych Cross Nurseries and Garden Centre*, located in the heart of Ashdown Forest, is a must for any gardening enthusiast (whether budding or firmly established). It has been going strong for 12 years now, building up its growing reputation as a major centre for roses: they stock nearly 500 varieties. This family-run, independent nursery also offers a superb range of herbaceous perennials, alpines and ornamental trees, as well as a large selection of shrubs and seasonal bedding plants. Owner Jim Plant and his friendly, knowledgeable staff are happy to advise on all matters horticultural. As well as the impressive assortment of plants, the nursery sells quality terracotta pots, hand-crafted garden furniture and a collection of unusual and high-quality garden features. The centre's coffee shop - 'The Hybrid Tea' - continues the rose theme. Regular customers wishing to join the nursery's Garden Club (membership currently 1,200 plus) receive newsletters, are invited to attend meetings, and of course receive a discount on all their purchases. *Wych Cross Nurseries and Garden Centre, Forest Row, East Sussex RH18 5JW Tel: 01342 822705.*

**Wych Cross Nurseries & Garden Centre**

## Fletching
*Map 3 ref L4*

*7 miles SW of Crowborough off the A272*

Fletching's pleasant main street contains a number of other noteworthy buildings, including Fletching Lodge, Corner Cottage and St Andrews House. The last named has a timbered upper floor which was added in the 19th century to match its older next-door neighbour and was once the family home of the Maryon-Wilson family, rival landowners to the Sheffields. On 5th November each year, people come from a wide area to join in the village Bonfire Night celebrations, a tradition which once had more sinister religious overtones. At the bottom of Fletching's main street, there is an imposing, though closed, stone gateway to Sheffield Park Gardens. St Mary and St Andrews' Church with its Norman spire is a notable landmark for the village. Historian Edward Gibbon, author of *The Decline and Fall of the Roman Empire*, is buried in the church mausoleum.

Just a mile further on from Fletching, *The Forge* bed and breakfast hotel occupies a beautiful timber-framed Queen-Anne style house. The centuries old toll booth outside marks its position at the edge of the historic, lovely old village of Fletching, near Uckfield. Owners Stewart and Joy Partridge are a convivial and pleasant couple who enjoy making every guest's stay a memorable one. The bedrooms are spacious and supremely comfortable. In winter there's a roaring log fire in the guests' lounge; in summer the gracious gar-

**The Forge**

den is filled with flowering plants and shrubs. The farmhouse breakfast provided is excellent, and there is an award-winning pub in the
village for evening meals. Guests with an interest in vintage cars
are in for a particular treat: Stewart owns the garage next door and
is a fount of knowledge on all aspects of vintage British motorcars.
There is good walking and birdwatching in this very quiet, charming area of East Sussex, and The Forge is ideally situated as a base
for touring the surrounding countryside. *The Forge, Splaynes Green,
Fletching, Uckfield, East Sussex TN22 3TL Tel: 01825 712960.*

## Newick                                    Map 3 ref L5
*8 miles SW of Crowborough off the A272*

This large and sprawling village is centred around a broad triangular green. On the green, there is an unusual village pump which
was erected to mark Queen Victoria's diamond jubilee in 1897.
Newick's other noteworthy features include the part-Norman St
Mary's Chuch with its Perpendicular sandstone tower, an Old Rectory with distinctive wrought-iron railings, Founthill House, and
the former Lady Vernon's School (now School Cottage) which was
founded in 1771 as a school for 'poor girls'. The actor Dirk Bogarde
was brought up in the area and was given his first big part in an
amateur production at Newick in the 1930s.

## Chailey                                   Map 3 ref K5
*9 miles SW of Crowborough off the A275*

Chailey is a large, scattered parish of three villages: North Chailey,
Chailey and South Common. Chairly has some impressive old buildings, including the 13th century St Peter's Church, a moated rec-

tory, a late 17th century residence, the Hooke, and a Georgian country house, Ades.

*Chailey Common* is a designated nature reserve, with 450 acres of wet and dry heathland, featuring a well preserved smock windmill. *Chailey Heritage* is a learning centre which was established in 1903 to instruct seven physically disabled children from the East End of London. It now has a roll of over 200 students and a worldwide reputation. It also has a highly individual Edwardian chapel which was designed by Sir Ninian Comper shortly before the First World War.

## Sheffield Park
*Map 3 ref L4*
*8 miles SW of Crowborough off the A275*

Sheffield Park is situated in the northeast corner of the parish of Chailey. The village takes its name from its manor house, a Tudor building remodelled in 1775 by James Wyatt for the Earl of Sheffield, it is best known for the 100 acre National Trust-owned *Sheffield Park Gardens*. During the late 18th century, the grounds of Sheffield Park were laid out in a grand style, at first by 'Capability' Brown and then by Humphry Repton, on the instructions of John

*Sheffield Par Gardens*

Baker Holroyd MP, the first Earl of Sheffield. At around the same time, he also commissioned James Wyatt to build **Sheffield Park House**, an impressive mansion which can be seen from a distance but is not open to the public. The third Earl of Sheffield was an enthusiastic cricketer who organised the first test tours of England by the Australians. He also established a tradition (which lasted only 20 years or so) where the Australian team would play the first match of their tour at Sheffield Park against an Earl of Sheffield's XI. The former cricket field, now studded with specimen trees and shrubs, can still be made out on a rise above the main lake.

The gardens lie within a steep sided valley and contain a series of five lakes with connecting cascades which were constructed over a period of 100 years. In spring, the ground is covered with bluebells and daffodils, in early summer there is a wonderful show of azaleas and rhododendrons, and later in the year, the autumn foliage creates a spectacular blaze of colour.

**Sheffield Park Station**, the southern terminus of the famous **Bluebell Railway** (the entrance is almost opposite Sheffield Park Gardens). This privately-owned stretch of the former East Grinstead to Lewes line runs for five miles through a delightful wooded valley which, as the name suggests, is carpeted with bluebells in springtime. One of the first of the new generation of private steam railways, the line was acquired by the Bluebell Railway Preservation Company in 1961 and is largely staffed by a team of dedicated volunteers.

The station dates from around 1882 and is undergoing an ongoing programme of restoration. The engine sheds house a unique collection of around 30 vintage locomotives, some of which are over 100 years old, and there is also a fascinating museum of railway memorabilia, a signal box, shops and a cafe. Those travelling to the northern terminus at Horsted Keynes will find an interesting collection of railway carriages and an attractive picnic area.

# Tourist Information Centres

*Centres in **bold** are open all the year around.*

### Arundel
*61 High Street, Arundel, West Sussex BN18 9AJ*
*Tel: 01903 882268 Fax: 01903 882419*

### Battle
*88 High Street, Battle, East Sussex TN33 9AQ*
*Tel: 01424 773721*

### Bexhill-on-Sea
*51 Marina, Bexhill-on-Sea, East Sussex TN40 1BQ*
*Tel: 01424 732208*

### Bognor Regis
*Belmont Street, Bognor Regis, West Sussex PO21 1BJ*
*Tel: 01243 823140*

### Boship
*Boship Roundabout A22, Lower Dicker, Hailsham*
*East Sussex BN27 4DT  Tel: 01323 442667*

### Brighton
*Bartholomew Square, Brighton, East Sussex BN1 1JS*
*Tel: 01273 323755*

### Chichester
*29a South Street, Chichester, West Sussex PO19 1AH*
*Tel: 01243 775888*

## Crowborough

*Tourism and Arts Section, Wealden District Council*
*Council Offices, Pine Grove, Crowborough, East Sussex*
*TN6 1DH  Tel: 01892 602000*

## Eastbourne

*Cornfield Road, Eastbourne, East Sussex BN21 4QL*
*Tel: 01323 411400*

## Fontwell

*Little Chef Complex, Fontwell, West Sussex BN18 0SD*
*Tel: 01243 543269*

## Gatwick

*Airport International Arrivals, East Grinstead*
*West Sussex RH6 0NP Tel: 01293 579102*

## Hailsham

*The Library, Western Road, Hailsham, East Sussex BN27 3DN*
*Tel: 01323 844426/840604*

## Hastings

*4 Robertson Terrace, Hastings, East Sussex TN34 1EZ*
*Tel: 01424 781111*

## Horsham

*9, The Causeway, Horsham West Sussex RH12 1HE*
*Tel: 01403 211661*

## Hove

*Church Road, Hove, East Sussex BN3 4AH*
*Tel: 01273 778087*

## Lewes

*187 High Street, Lewes, East Sussex BN7 2DE*
*Tel: 01273 483448*

## Littlehampton

*Windmill Complex, Littlehampton, West Sussex BN17 5LH*
*Tel: 01903 713480*

## Midhurst

*North Street, Midhurst, West Sussex GU29 9DW*
*Tel: 01730 817322*

### Petworth

*Market Square, Petworth, West Sussex GU28 0AF*
*Tel: 01798 343523*

### Pevensey

*Castle Cottage, Pevensey, East Sussex BN24 5LE*
*Tel: 01323 761444*

### Rye

*The Heritage Centre, Strand Quay, Rye, East Sussex TN31 7AY*
*Tel: 01797 226696*

### Seaford

*Station Approach, Seaford, East Sussex BN25 2AR*
*Tel: 01323 897426*

### Shoreham

*Civic Centre, Main Road, Shoreham-by-Sea*
*West Sussex BN43 6PR  Tel: 01273 455566*

### Worthing

*Chapel Road, Worthing, West Sussex BN11 1HL*
*Tel: 01903 210022*

The Hidden Places of Sussex

# Index

# I

# J

# K

# L

# M

# N

## The Hidden Places Series

# ORDERFORM

To order more copies of this title or any of the others in this series
please complete the order form below and send to:

**Travel Publishing Ltd,7a Apollo House, Calleva Park
Aldermaston, Berks, RG7 8TN**

|  | Price | Quantity | Value |
|---|---|---|---|
| **Regional Titles** | | | |
| Channel Islands | £6.99 | ............ | ............ |
| Cheshire | £7.99 | ............ | ............ |
| Cornwall | £7.99 | ............ | ............ |
| Devon | £7.99 | ............ | ............ |
| Dorset, Hants & Isle of Wight | £4.95 | ............ | ............ |
| Gloucestershire | £6.99 | ............ | ............ |
| Heart of England | £4.95 | ............ | ............ |
| Kent | £7.99 | ............ | ............ |
| Lake District & Cumbria | £4.95 | ............ | ............ |
| Lancashire | £7.99 | ............ | ............ |
| Norfolk | £7.99 | ............ | ............ |
| Northeast Yorkshire | £6.99 | ............ | ............ |
| Northumberland & Durham | £6.99 | ............ | ............ |
| Nottinghamshire | £6.99 | ............ | ............ |
| Peak District | £6.99 | ............ | ............ |
| Potteries | £6.99 | ............ | ............ |
| Somerset | £6.99 | ............ | ............ |
| South East | £4.95 | ............ | ............ |
| South Wales | £4.95 | ............ | ............ |
| Surrey | £6.99 | ............ | ............ |
| Suffolk | £7.99 | ............ | ............ |
| Sussex | £6.99 | ............ | ............ |
| Thames & Chilterns | £5.99 | ............ | ............ |
| Welsh Borders | £5.99 | ............ | ............ |
| Wiltshire | £6.99 | ............ | ............ |
| Yorkshire Dales | £6.99 | ............ | ............ |
| **Set of any 5 Regional titles** | **£25.00** | ............ | ............ |
| **National Titles** | | | |
| England | £9.99 | ............ | ............ |
| Ireland | £8.99 | ............ | ............ |
| Scotland | £8.99 | ............ | ............ |
| Wales | £8.99 | ............ | ............ |
| **Set of all 4 National titles** | **£28.00** | ............ | ............ |
| | **TOTAL** | _____ | _____ |

**For orders of less than 4 copies please add £1 per book for
postage & packing. Orders over 4 copies P & P free.**

### PLEASE TURN OVER TO COMPLETE
### PAYMENT DETAILS

# *The Hidden Places Series*
# *ORDER FORM*

## Please complete following details:

### I wish to pay for this order by:

Cheque: ☐          Switch: ☐

Access: ☐          Visa: ☐

### Either:

Card No: ☐☐☐☐ ☐☐☐☐ ☐☐☐☐ ☐☐☐☐

Expiry Date: ☐☐ ☐☐

Signature: ..................................................................

### Or:

I enclose a cheque for £ ......................... made payable to Travel Publishing Ltd

NAME: ........................................................................

ADDRESS: ........................................................................

........................................................................

........................................................................

........................................................................

POSTCODE: ........................................................................

TEL NO: ........................................................................

**Please send to:**     Travel Publishing Ltd
7a Apollo House
Calleva Park
Aldermaston
Berks, RG7 8TN

# *The Hidden Places Series*
# READER REACTION FORM

**The Hidden Places** research team would like to receive reader's comments on any visitor attractions or places reviewed in the book and also recommendations for suitable entries to be included in the next edition. This will help ensure that the **Hidden Places** series continues to provide its readers with useful information on the more interesting, unusual or unique features of each attraction or place ensuring that their stay in the local area is an enjoyable and stimulating experience.

To provide your comments or recommendations would you please complete the forms below as indicated and send to: **The Research Department, Travel Publishing Ltd., 7a Apollo House, Calleva Park, Aldermaston, Reading, RG7 8TN.**

Please tick as appropriate: Comments ☐ Recommendation ☐

Name of *"Hidden Place"*:

Address:

Telephone Number:

Name of Contact:

Comments/Reason for recommendation:

Name of Reader:

Address:

Telephone Number:

# *The Hidden Places Series*
# **READER REACTION FORM**

*The Hidden Places* research team would like to receive reader's comments on any visitor attractions or places reviewed in the book and also recommendations for suitable entries to be included in the next edition. This will help ensure that the *Hidden Places* series continues to provide its readers with useful information on the more interesting, unusual or unique features of each attraction or place ensuring that their stay in the local area is an enjoyable and stimulating experience.

To provide your comments or recommendations would you please complete the forms below as indicated and send to: **The Research Department, Travel Publishing Ltd., 7a Apollo House, Calleva Park, Aldermaston, Reading, RG7 8TN.**

Please tick as appropriate:    Comments ☐    Recommendation ☐

Name of *"Hidden Place"*:

Address:

Telephone Number:

Name of Contact:

Comments/Reason for recommendation:

Name of Reader:

Address:

Telephone Number:

# *The Hidden Places Series*
# READER REACTION FORM

*The Hidden Places* research team would like to receive reader's comments on any visitor attractions or places reviewed in the book and also recommendations for suitable entries to be included in the next edition. This will help ensure that the *Hidden Places* series continues to provide its readers with useful information on the more interesting, unusual or unique features of each attraction or place ensuring that their stay in the local area is an enjoyable and stimulating experience.

To provide your comments or recommendations would you please complete the forms below as indicated and send to: **The Research Department, Travel Publishing Ltd., 7a Apollo House, Calleva Park, Aldermaston, Reading, RG7 8TN.**

Please tick as appropriate: Comments ☐ Recommendation ☐

Name of *"Hidden Place"*:

Address:

Telephone Number:

Name of Contact:

Comments/Reason for recommendation:

Name of Reader:

Address:

Telephone Number:

# *The Hidden Places Series*
# READER REACTION FORM

*The Hidden Places* research team would like to receive reader's comments on any visitor attractions or places reviewed in the book and also recommendations for suitable entries to be included in the next edition. This will help ensure that the *Hidden Places* series continues to provide its readers with useful information on the more interesting, unusual or unique features of each attraction or place ensuring that their stay in the local area is an enjoyable and stimulating experience.

To provide your comments or recommendations would you please complete the forms below as indicated and send to: **The Research Department, Travel Publishing Ltd., 7a Apollo House, Calleva Park, Aldermaston, Reading, RG7 8TN.**

Please tick as appropriate: Comments ☐ Recommendation ☐

Name of *"Hidden Place"*:

Address:

Telephone Number:

Name of Contact:

Comments/Reason for recommendation:

Name of Reader:

Address:

Telephone Number:

# Map Section

The following pages of maps encompass the main cities, towns and geographical features of both East and West Sussex, as well as all the many interesting places featured in the guide. Distances are indicated by the use of scale bars located below each of the maps

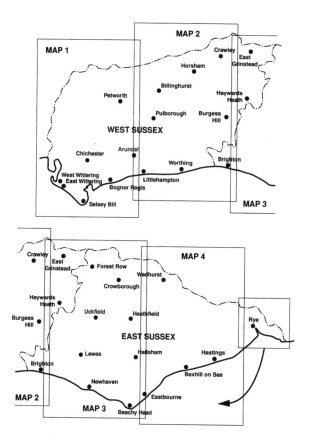

These maps are small scale extracts from the *Sussex & Surrey Official Tourist Map,* reproduced with kind permission of *Estates Publications.*

*The Hidden Places of Sussex*

*250*